What Do International Students Think and Feel?

Adapting to U.S. College Life and Culture

JERRY G. GEBHARD

ANN ARBOR
University of Michigan Press

This book is dedicated to the memory of my parents,
Homer & Margaret Gebhard,
who inspired me to be curious about people and culture.

Copyright © by the University of Michigan 2010
All rights reserved
Published in the United States of America
The University of Michigan Press
Manufactured in the United States of America

∞ Printed on acid-free paper

ISBN-13: 978-0-472-03406-2

2013   2012   2011   2010   4 3   2   1

Library of Congress Cataloging-in-Publication Data

Gebhard, Jerry Greer.
    What do international students think and feel? : adapting to U.S. college life and culture / Jerry G. Gebhard.
        p. cm.
    Includes bibliographical references.
    ISBN 978-0-472-03406-2 (pbk. : alk. paper) 1.   Students, Foreign—United States—Attitudes—Case Studies. 2.   Students, Foreign—United States—Social conditions—Case studies. 3.   College students—United States—Attitudes—Case studies. 4.   College students—United States—Social conditions—Case studies. 5.   Education, Higher—Social aspects—United States—Case studies. I.   Title.
    LB2376.4.G43 2010
    378.1'9826910973—dc22   2010022207

Acknowledgments

First, I give my heartfelt thanks to all of the international students and Americans who participated in this project. Although I could only include a fraction of the interviews and written narratives in this book, it would not have been possible without the generous cooperation they all extended in sharing their experiences and impressions.

I also want to express my sincere gratitude to graduate student assistants and others who did library research, interviewed international students, provided emic (insider's) perspective on international student cultural adaptation processes, issues, and strategies, as well as offered feedback on the selection of narratives and chapters in this book. Special thanks go to Pisarn Chamcharatsri, Tim Conrad, Joel Diamond, Anestine Hector, Milcah Ochieng, Deepak Pant, Massaer Paye, Sandra Salinko, Soo-Jeong Shin, Maria Saryusz-Szarska, Theresa Tseng, Chaoboo Wang, Zhiling Wu, Weier Ye, and Qisi Zhang. I also thank Lydia Giles, Anestine Hector, David Purnell, and Reed Venrick for inviting me to direct their doctoral dissertations on cultural adaptation processes as I was able to more clearly understand my own research through our mutually rewarding conversations.

I also want to thank Ted Chan for his talented editing work, as well as Kelly Sippell and the dedicated staff at the University of Michigan Press for their advice, patience, and skilled editing.

Last but not least, I want to thank my wife, Yoko Kato Gebhard, for her patience, support, understanding, and love.

Contributors

As a part of the human subject contract with the many international students and Americans who contributed spoken or written narratives to this book, I promised not to disclose their names along with their narratives. However, without matching name with contribution, I want to acknowledge everyone who contributed either a narrative or a quote. The contributors, in alphabetical order by last name, include:

Mubarak Alkhatnai
Adel Alomrani
Yuko Asano
Motcho Atchade
So Young Baek
Maria Luciana Beltramo
Chin-hui Chen
Mei-yu Chen
Vachraeeporn Chuapaknam
Susan Finlayson
Joshua Gordon
Eun-hee Han
Anestine Hector
Leohardt Hesse
Jo-Hsi Hu
Richard Kanda
Roza Kazakbaeva
Won-Hyeong Kim
Imam Kolaemi
Moses Kwatzo
Noh-Shin Lee

Xiaoping Li
Gandah Nabi Mahamadou
Chandrika Mehta
Amy Moretti
Leroy Muya
Daisy Muhavi Nyangah
Yuji Ogura
David Purnell
Asma Rammal
So-Jeong Shin
Alvin Smith
Akiko Suzuka
Marisol Tellez
Chisato Tomobe
Mila Veshcherevich
Nataporn Wathiwutipong
Szu-Ying Wu
Xiaojing Yang
Alexandria Yunadi
Faishal Zakaria

Contents

Introduction

What Can Be Discovered from Reading This Book

What Do International Students Think and Feel? seeks to illuminate the lives of international students at colleges and universities in the United States. The goal of this book is to build the readers' awareness about what it means to adjust to another culture. The book, which is based on more than two decades of ongoing inquiry into the cultural adjustment process of international students studying in U.S. university language institutes and undergraduate and graduate programs, features a rich and varied assortment of personal narratives shared through the years by international students from countries all over the world.

These narratives include accounts of international students' dreams and goodbyes before moving to the United States to study; their initial experiences soon after arriving; their increasing involvement with Americans* in and outside the classroom; and the myriad problems, issues, and challenges they encounter. This book is also about strategies that international students use to navigate a new culture—strategies that succeed and fail. It also includes accounts of students' experiences as they return to their homeland and have to readjust to their home culture—accounts that describe both the problems they face and also the awareness they have gained about themselves and their cultural values and behaviors.

---

*We are using *Americans* throughout this book because it is the term generally applied to people who live in the United States, even though we are aware that people living in other countries are also Americans. In this book, we are using it to refer only to people who live in the United States.

What Do International Students Think and Feel? includes narratives from international students from many different countries, including China, Japan, Korea, Thailand, Taiwan, Indonesia, Malaysia, Vietnam, Kazakhstan, Russia, Saudi Arabia, Jordan, Iraq, Egypt, Syria, Pakistan, India, Kenya, Benin, Niger, Nigeria, Grenada, Cuba, Argentina, Colombia, Costa Rica, Germany, England, France, Italy, Hungary, Poland, and other countries. Through these personal narratives, readers can hear about the cultural adjustment process of international students in their own words.

Who Can Benefit from Reading This Book

The primary audience for this book is students who are studying in TESOL programs in North America. This book can be used in an Introduction to TESOL class, an Intercultural Communication class, or any course that incorporates the cultural adaptation experiences of international students in the United States. This book can also be valuable to ESL teachers who are teaching at language institutes, university liberal arts programs with international students, or other courses and programs with an international student population.

What Do International Students Think and Feel? can be useful as part of an international student orientation program and as a resource in an international center. Newly arrived students can benefit from hearing the perspectives of international students who have preceded them. The book can help students gain an understanding of the basic process of adaptation, consider their own issues related to cultural adaptation, and weigh suitable approaches to their new surroundings.

This book can also be used as part of a program outside the United States to prepare university exchange, scholarship, and other program students and professionals who plan to study and live in the United States. Most programs that prepare people to study abroad typically offer them opportunities to strengthen their academic reading, writing, listening, and speaking skills. This book will add another needed skill area—understanding the concepts of cultural values, behaviors, perceptions, and strategies related to cultural adaptation.

Because one of the aims of this book is to reveal what it means to be an international student through the perspectives of students on a university campus, this book could be adapted to any academic course that seeks to sensitize American undergraduate and graduate students to the lives of international students. It could also be a catalyst for American students (and teachers/professors) not only to expand their perceptions about the lives of international students, but also to become more involved in supporting them as they face culturally based academic and social challenges.

 ## Qualitative Research: Design and Methodology

This book is based on more than twenty years of research into the lives of international students studying at American colleges and universities. From the beginning of this project, I was fortunate to work with graduate assistants, and over the years I trained and worked with both American and international students (from China, Ghana, Grenada, Hungary, India, Kenya, Korea, Poland, Nepal, Senegal, Taiwan, and Thailand). Some of these research assistants, who are acknowledged on page v, worked with me for several years and were invaluable. They were able to elicit deeply moving stories (narratives) from classmates, friends, and themselves about their cultural adaptation experiences. Although I also developed close trusting relationships with a variety of international students and gained privileged access to stories about their lives, some of the international student researchers, as insiders, were able to gain greater access to cultures and people.

We used a Qualitative Research design and methodology, making use of a variety of sources and research experiences (Agar, 1980, 1996; Baker, 2004; Bogdan & Biklen, 2006; Denzin & Lincoln, 1994, 2005; Emerson, Fretz, & Shaw, 1995; Lincoln, 1995; Maxwell, 2004; Pagnucci, 2004; Richards, 2003; Rubin & Rubin, 2004; Rule & Wheeler, 2000;

Spradely, 1979) to understand the cultural adaptation experiences of the international students. The research was conducted at several universities in the students' natural settings, such as in university dorms, libraries, classrooms, cafeterias, international student clubs, and Internet chat rooms, as well as in supermarkets, coffee shops, apartments, subways, and other places on and off campus that international students frequent.

The goal of our research was to describe, analyze, and consider multiple interpretations of what the descriptions might mean (Fanselow, 1988, 1997). We collected descriptions through a variety of qualitative research techniques, including conversations with international students and their teachers and friends over time (some over months), informal structured interviews (taped), and group discussions. We also asked students to write essays and short stories about their cultural adaptation experiences, had ongoing email correspondence with some, and kept field notes on observations of international students as they circulated in the university community.

I analyzed the collection of descriptions over time, and coupled with a review of the literature (Gebhard, 2010), I was able to understand and categorize the experiences of the international students, as well as identify complexity and issues within the adaptation process (Part 3). I was also able to recognize and categorize international student behaviors that seemed to impede successful adaptation (Part 4), as well as strategies that seem to work for them (Part 5).

As a part of the research process, my research assistants and I asked each person to complete a Human Subjects Consent Form that granted permission to publish their narratives. As a part of this human subject contract between the students and me, I promised not to disclose their names along with their narratives.

 How This Book Is Organized

What Do International Students Think and Feel? includes six themes or parts. Part 1, Challenges International Students Face, explores the types of challenges that confront international students as they attempt to adapt to a different culture (Chapter 1). This first chapter also provides a foundation for gaining a deeper understanding of the themes and narratives in Parts 2–6.

Part 2, The Basic Phases of Cultural Adaptation, includes five chapters, each one describing a different phase of cultural adjustment. The phases include preparing to leave the home country for the United States (Chapter 2), initial experiences in the United States (Chapter 3), increasing interaction and challenges (Chapter 4), culture shock (Chapter 5), and adaptation to life in the United States (Chapter 6). Each chapter presents adaptation narratives told through the words of the international students or the Americans who interact with them.

Part 3, Beyond Phases: The Complexity of Cultural Adaptation, explains why cultural adaptation should not simply be understood as a series of phases. One reason is because cultural adaptation is a dynamic process; international students do not necessarily move from one phase to the next in a linear progression. For example, some students have culture shock soon after arriving, while others believe they have successfully adjusted initially, only to find themselves regressing to an earlier phase (Chapter 7). Cultural adaptation is also complex because international students continue to have value conflicts and identity issues even after being in the United States for some time (Chapter 8).

Part 4, Behavior That Can Encumber Successful Adaptation, highlights behaviors that some international students have used that are not conducive to successfully adjusting to a new culture, such as complaining and avoiding interactions with Americans (Chapter 9), and expecting Americans to adapt to the international student's home-culture way of interacting, and withdrawing into the expatriate community (Chapter 10).

Part 5, Strategies and Successful Adaptation, contains four chapters on strategies that international students find useful in adapting to the university and larger community culture. These strategies include using humor and optimism (Chapter 11), using observation and matching behaviors (Chapter 12), doing and reflecting (Chapter 13), and finding support (Chapter 14).

Part 6, Home Again—Readapting and Reflections on Living Abroad, includes international students' reflections on their experiences in the

United States. Narratives include the types of problems and difficult decisions that international students face when they return home (Chapter 15) and the awareness and understanding that they have gained (Chapter 16).

Each of the six parts ends with a set of Reflective Questions for readers to consider. These questions are provided in the interest of provoking reflection and discussion. Readers can answer these questions alone or share answers with other readers as a stimulus for further considering the book's narratives and six themes.

A Note about the Author's Intentions

My intention in writing this book is to illuminate the lives of international students who are studying at colleges and universities in the United States and, through their narratives, to build readers' awareness about what it means to adapt to another culture. My intention is in no way to imply that international students should try to become acculturated into the United States.

A Note about the Narratives: Voice and Editing

I have done my best to maintain the original voices of the international students and other participants within each of the narratives included in this book. While some international students used English at a very advanced level, others' use of English was more basic, and most students' English was somewhere in between. As a result, when the intended meaning of the student was not clear, I attempted to clarify the English without changing the original meaning.

Readers are invited to sit with these students to learn about their experiences in living and studying in the United States.

PART 1

Challenges International Students Face

Part 1 examines the many challenges that international students face when they move to the United States to study at a university or college. Challenges include adapting to a new physical setting, using English within a culturally different academic system, interacting socially, handling emotional problems, and creating and using adaptation strategies. Part 1 also introduces the five cultural adaptation themes that will be explored in more detail through the narratives in Parts 2 to 6.

CHAPTER 1

Adapting to University Life and the Larger Community Culture

Through our explorations into the lives of international students at U.S. universities, my research assistants and I discovered the obvious: international students face many challenges. In addition to adapting to new climate, food, and surroundings, students must also adjust to a U.S. academic system in which professors assume, to varying degrees, that international students are literate enough in English to comprehend the material in textbooks and other readings; follow lectures; interact with classmates and the professor in seminars; take exams; do library research; and write academic papers. International students are also confronted with a barrage of settings in which they are expected to interact with Americans* in culturally different ways. Such interactions seem especially challenging to international students who do not yet realize that American students, both within and outside the university setting, are not necessarily alike in their values and behavior.

For some students, the persistent demand to adapt can lead to an unexpected range of emotions, including frustration, anxiety, confusion, homesickness, and depression. These feelings need to be addressed and

*We are using *Americans* throughout this book because it is the term generally applied to people who live in the United States, even though we are aware that people living in other countries are also Americans. In this book, we are using it to refer only to people who live in the United States.

resolved, creating yet another set of challenges to their new life as international students.

Challenges Adapting to a New Physical Setting

Most of the students we interviewed said that, initially, they felt thrilled to be in the United States and that their new surroundings were filled with interesting things to see and do. The new surroundings, however, also complicated their lives as they needed to locate buildings and classrooms, banks, stores, and more. What was once a fairly simple thing to do in their homeland became a problem. For example, a student from Indonesia said that he missed his first class because he went to the wrong classroom (ten minutes early), sat in the front row, didn't realize he was in the wrong room until after the class started, and didn't want to disrupt the professor or embarrass himself by leaving. Another student from Japan went to a local supermarket to buy big towels: "I asked the store clerk where is the second floor to buy bath towel. She smiled and said, 'We don't have second floor, and we don't sell towels.' I was so embarrassed. In Japan we can buy big towel and many other things on the second floor of a small supermarket."

Another challenge was living in a dormitory, an experience that is often new for American and international students alike. As some students pointed out, dorms tend to be noisy and crowded with students eating together in a large cafeteria, often playing loud music, and forming and re-forming new friendships. A number of international students pointed out that the language and cultural rules for interacting in American dorms were unexpectedly different. For example, some international students from cultures where shyness about nudity is valued were surprised that some American students are not bashful about nudity in dorm rooms or shower areas. (Chapter 10 describes life in a typical U.S. undergraduate dormitory and the problems this created for one Thai student.)

The adjustment of living in a university or off-campus dorm can be even more stressful for older international students, many of whom reported that they missed their apartments or houses in their home countries. Here is what an older student from Germany told me about her problem adjusting to a dorm: "I am not used to such a place. I can't sleep or concentrate. I keep hearing the loud TV in the next room, laughing and conversations in the hallways, and doors opening and shutting."

Most international students said they looked forward to experiencing a new climate, but as Storti (2001) points out, climate can affect one's body, health, lifestyle, pocketbook, and mind. International students from tropical climates, for example, who chose to study in northern U.S. states divulged that they wanted to experience winter and the dramatic beauty of seasonal changes. They all said they enjoyed the colorful autumn and the first snowfall, but, as the snow continued and the winter turned colder and colder, some international students grumbled about wearing coats and hats. Some complained that it was too warm and restrictive inside buildings; that they couldn't sleep well in heated rooms; and that they caught colds easily and felt depressed during the cold, dark days and nights. For example, a student from Thailand moaned, "I thought winter would be fun. But, not fun. It's too dark and cold. I feel sad too much." Still, other students rarely griped and said they enjoyed the beauty of different seasons.

Most students expected to have some problems with American food, but many were surprised by how difficult it was to get used to it. Some students who ate in the college cafeteria said that the food was a novelty at first, but after a few weeks, the food became boring and problematic. As one student pointed out, "I like the fried chicken, the salad bar, and the milk shake. But, the food is always same, and to me no taste. I am hungry for food with spices from my country." Another student shook his head in disgust when he told me, "The food makes me physically ill. Even the smell makes me sick." Of course, not all international students had such problems. As another student told me, "I have no problem with food. It tastes okay, and there are a lot of choices. But, I am getting fat!"

English Language Challenges in Academic Settings

One problem that came as a surprise to some international students was the challenge of academic reading. International students, many of whom were from Asian countries, consistently reported that it took them a long time to read class assignments. As a student from Vietnam explained, "In Vietnam we learn to read English word by word, line by line. We translate and analyze every word. I think it helps us to understand meaning, but also we take a long time to read something."

The amount of required reading was also an issue, especially for graduate students who had to read many textbooks, journal articles, and professor handouts. As one graduate student expressed, "In Korea the professor only uses one book. We read that book very carefully, and the professor lectures on that book. Here I have to read many books and articles, and content is very difficult. It is a big problem."

Another academic challenge was writing. Many international students articulated that they were not prepared for the demands of taking essay exams and writing research papers. A graduate student from Hungary put it this way: "In Hungary we don't write many papers really, not like here in the U.S. We read and listen to lectures, but we might have oral exams. I can easily talk about what I study, but when I have to write it down, everything slows down, especially when I have to write a formal library research paper." An undergraduate from Japan explained the problem with writing in this way: "I have lot of anxiety about writing in English. I am afraid to make mistakes." (In Chapter 14, a Taiwanese student describes her experiences with writing assignments.)

Some international students also found professors' lectures and seminars difficult when they first arrived. To summarize what many students said about their lecture experiences: Some professors were highly organized, used PowerPoint presentations, and moved systematically from one point to the next, while others talked freely and spontaneously and sometimes jumped from one point to the next and then back again to a previous point. Related to this problem, a student from Poland expressed her concern in this way: "I kept listening. But, I couldn't understand very much, and my notes a mess. A lot of words and no meaning. Later I realized that this professor, he likes to tell jokes and stories in the middle of his lecture."

Some international students found smaller seminars quite challenging because they were expected to talk in class with the professor and classmates. Many students, especially from Asian countries, said they had little experience with such classroom interaction. A student from Indonesia put it this way: "I was so surprised. I mean people at international student orientation told me that American professors like students to talk in class, but I really did not expect students to give an opinion and even challenge the professor." (Chapter 4 reveals how a student from Taiwan struggles with speaking in class. Chapter 13 shows how a student from Japan overcame her fears of talking in class.)

Communication Challenges in Social Settings

In addition to the language challenges associated with academics, a number of international students have said how surprised, disappointed, and anxious they were about their inability to socially interact with Americans when they first arrived. Related to comprehending spoken English, one student stated, "My new American roommate started talking really fast. I couldn't understand anything she said after, 'Hi. I'm Nancy.' It was like I have never heard English before!" (Chapter 3 illustrates a Taiwanese student's realization that she has listening comprehension problems.)

Some international students expressed their trouble with understanding accents, including southern accents and English accents of students from other countries. A few students pointed out they had difficulty decoding the linking of sounds, as in the way Americans say, *Why don't you find out?* When said in natural conversation, as a student from Japan jokingly said, "The pronunciation of *find out* sounded just like

find doubt. I wondered, why does the person want me to *find doubt?*"
Such comprehension problems can also affect students who grew up
speaking English in their daily lives. As a student from India articulated,
"I grew up hearing British English spoken with an Indian accent. I was
very surprised when I could not understand the American accent. I had
to listen carefully."

In addition to listening problems while communicating with
Americans, some students realized they had difficulties with the social-
cultural rules for appropriate behavior within a given social setting. For
example, several Asian students admitted they had felt uncomfortable
wearing shoes in the house when they lived with or visited American
families. A Thai student reported that she felt like she was making the
house dirty and constantly wanted to free her feet from the discomfort
of her shoes. (Chapter 4 reveals how a Japanese home-stay student
resolved the problem of wearing shoes in the house.)

Another example of social-cultural challenges is illustrated by a
Korean student who expressed how surprised she was when her American
friend told her not to be so negative when someone complements her. This
student was confronted with her own home-culture impulse to react to
a complement with humility by denying the complement (Kohls, 1996).
She reacted with, "Oh no, I'm such a poor student" when complemented
on her excellent grades rather than with, "thank you" (Wolfson,
1986).

Many international students, at least those who socially interacted
with Americans, indicated that they were able to adapt to the social-
cultural differences through their daily experiences. However, most said
that it took a lot of interaction to master the subtle cues or communicative
signposts that guide Americans through communication in an appropriate way.

As Weaver (2000b) points out, social cues can be in the form of words
or nonverbal behavior (gestures, facial expressions, postures), and they
tell us many things: when and how to give gifts; whether to be serious or
humorous; how to complement and react to complements; if it is accept-
able to interrupt a speaker and how to speak to leaders and subordinates;

when to shake hands; how to ask questions, invite someone to a party, turn down an invitation, make appointments, use titles and names, take off shoes in a home, and give and open a present—and much more. (Chapter 3 shows how a Briton has trouble understanding classroom cues to answer the professor's questions. Chapter 4 shows how a student from Hong Kong learned cultural cues related to taking phone messages during her home stay. Chapter 12 shows how a Japanese student learned the cues for laughing and applauding at a comedy show, as well as how a student from Argentina learned the subtle nonverbal cues used when walking through a crowd. Chapter 13 illustrates how a student from China learned the cues related to when and how to give and open a gift during a visit to an American home.)

 ## Emotional Challenges

As previously discussed, when the international students in our study first arrived, they were confronted with the challenges of adapting to a new physical setting, to a different academic system and accompanying language problems, as well as adapting to social interaction with Americans, including adjusting to new cultural cues and a myriad of strange, even ambiguous and unpredictable ways of doing things. Consequently, after a few weeks some students became physically and emotionally drained, in a state of disequilibrium, and with feelings of uncertainty, confusion, and anxiety (Adler, 1975; Begley, 2006; M.J. Bennett, 1998; Gebhard, 1987, 2006; Storti, 1989).

As a language institute student from El Salvador told me tearfully, "I am tired. Very tired. Bad humor. Now I have two month here. I want to go home. Tired." Another student from France simply said, "One minute I am happy, and the next minute I am sad or angry." (Chapter 5 provides a narrative on how a Malaysian student became moody and depressed. Chapter 5 also shows how a married student from India became anxious, even to the point of paranoia.)

Challenges with Encumbering Behavior

Sometimes students behave in ways that make adaptation difficult. For example, some of the international students we observed complained frequently about food, weather, noisy dorms, restaurants, American behavior, and many other things during their first months in the United States. While such complaining is an expected part of early adaptation and diminishes over time (Adler, 1975; Oberg, 1960; Storti, 2001; Weaver, 2000b), we discovered that a few students continued to complain excessively, and such students seemed to be especially challenged with adapting to American university life and culture. (Chapter 8 shows how a confused student from Kenya both praises and complains about Americans after having been in the United States for over a year. Chapter 9 includes a narrative from a German student who complains that conversations with Americans lack substance.)

Some international students react to cultural adaptation stress by withdrawing into a community made up of people from their own or similar cultures. Such withdraw, as Storti (1989, 2001) relates, provides a sanctuary for international students, but if such students continue to find refuge with others from their own cultural background, they miss opportunities to adapt more fully to life and culture at the university and local community, something that many international students in our study said they wanted to experience. (Chapter 10 shows how a Thai student's dream to have American friends is spoiled by her first experience with an immature American roommate and results in her flight to the security of the Thai community. Chapter 9 illustrates how a student from Benin withdrew by living alone and avoiding contact with Americans and other international students.)

Some international students used an *ethnocentric impulse* (Storti, 2001)—interacting with people in the host culture (at a conscious or unconscious level) through a notion that their own cultural values and ways of interacting are the correct or best way. Other students are not ethnocentric but use a *home-culture* way of interacting with Americans that can create misunderstanding. Students who adopted these approaches seemed to have much more difficulty adapting to university life. (Chapter 10 shows how a Nigerian student expects Americans to adapt to his values and ways of interacting. Chapter 10 also shows how a Chinese student is confused by her friend's reaction after using an indirect way of turning down an American classmate's invitation to a party.)

However, as international students face language, communication, and emotional challenges, most are able to get beyond complaining, avoiding, withdrawing, and expecting others to be like them, and they accept another kind of challenge—that of creating strategies that will help them to adapt.

Strategic Challenges

The international students in our study used a variety of useful adaptation strategies. One strategy that seemed to help a number of students is the use of humor. Some students who were suffering from homesickness and other symptoms of culture shock had the ability to laugh things off, a strategy that Kohls (1996) calls the ultimate weapon against despair. Others used humor more playfully as a way to enjoy their lives. Some students joked about the cold or hot humid weather, the food, and even at themselves for their intercultural communication faux pas. A Costa Rican student showed her humor in this way: "I laughed when my friend told me I turn guys on because I stand close to them and touch their arms. You know, in Costa Rica we can do this with friends, but standing and touching like that can give the wrong idea to guys here. My friend and I laugh because we know we have a little power to control guys here! But, we also have to be careful, you know." (Chapter 11 shows how a married couple from Syria had a playful humorous experience with an American boy at a shopping mall.)

Another, creative strategy that some students used to adapt was to observe and imitate Americans. Many students reported that they observed the way American students eat, walk on crowded streets, chat at coffee shops, greet each other, enter a classroom late, sit in class, interrupt each other, take a turn in a group discussion, and more. A few students took their observations further by matching the behaviors of Americans they observed. (Chapter 12 shows how a student from Argentina observes and imitates Americans' way of walking and eating, as well as how a Japanese student gains a new perspective on laughter by imitating Americans at a comedy show.)

A number of students acknowledged they used reflection as a strategy to adapt. After experiencing interaction with Americans, such as with a professor at her office or with a host family during a meal, they would take the time to reflect on what happened, how they felt about the interactive experience, and what they might do the same or differently next time. (Chapter 8 discloses how a student from Grenada gained a new perspective through reflection on what it means to be fat in America. Chapter 13 confirms the helpfulness of reflection for a Taiwanese student-boarder who is able to alter her social-interactive behavior, as well as for a South Korean student who gains awareness of his unfair narrow attitude toward African-Americans. Chapter 13 also reveals how a Japanese student is able to join class discussions by reflecting on her own behavior in class.)

The Cultural Adaptation Themes in This Book

Through my observations of international students over the years and in my analysis of their narratives, five distinct cultural adaptation themes have emerged. These themes are discussed and illustrated by the narratives in Parts 2–6 of this book.

Each theme provides a different understanding of cultural adaptation that can be used by pre-service and in-service teachers to gain empathy with ESL students studying in the United States and international students in undergraduate and graduate TESOL or related programs, as well as with other international students on campus. These five themes can be used by both American and international students to expand awareness of international students' lives, as well as to spark interest in establishing friendships.

Theme One: The Basic Phases of Cultural Adaptation

The first theme (Part 2, Chapters 2–6) centers on the basic phases of cultural adaptation, highlighting how each cultural adaptation phase builds on the previous one. Cultural adjustment is a process without definite borders; not all students progress through the phases in the same order and some students do not pass through a particular stage. But there is a general pattern to the phases, and most international students go through the phases in a common order.

These phases are based on my assistants and my qualitative inquiry into the lives of international students, as well as on a synthesis of ideas from the work of Adler (1975), Begley (2006), J.M. Bennett (1998), DeCapua & Wintergerst (2004), Lewis & Jungman (1986), Lysgarrd (1955), Oberg (1960), Storti (2001), and Weaver (2000b). We have indentified five basic phases of adaptation: (1) getting ready to leave, (2) initial experiences, (3) increasing interaction, (4) culture shock, and (5) adaptation.

Theme Two: The Complexity of Cultural Adaptation

The second theme (Part 3, Chapters 7–8) focuses on the complexity of cultural adaptation by looking at two specific issues. The first complexity involves the nonlinear way that many international students adjust and adapt to their new surroundings. Some students regress to earlier phases or go through more of a recursive process of adaptation (DeCapua & Wintergerst, 2004; Gebhard, 2001; Giles, 1996; Purnell, 2000). Such findings contradict the more linear way that cultural adaptation is often discussed, and hopefully, by studying the narratives in Chapter 7, those who oversimplify the phases will reconsider their stance.

The complexity of cultural adaptation can also be understood through the variety of issues that surface for international students during their lives in the United States (DeCapua & Wintergerst, 2004; Furnham & Bochner, 1986; Storti, 1989, 2001; Weaver, 2000b). For example, Storti (2001) raises the point that some individuals are faced with ethical or moral dilemmas. Some international students feel violated or confused by some Americans' behavior because it contradicts values fundamental to their identity. This became evident during my research when many of the female international students (and many American students) said they disliked and even felt repulsed when their American roommates invited their boyfriends to spend the night. Some said how embarrassing and annoying it was to have to try to sleep in the same room. (See Chapter 13 for a narrative about a Columbian student's experience.)

The major issues that emerged through my research centered on identity, race, time, being overweight, and stereotyping. The narratives in Chapter 8 can help American and international students, and others who are interested in the lives of international students, gain a deeper understanding of the kinds of issues that exist and how international students think and feel about these issues.

Theme Three: Behavior That Can Encumber Adaptation

The third theme (Part 4, Chapters 9–10) focuses on behaviors that seem to impede international students' chances of adapting to university life and culture. As discussed earlier, a few students complain in excess. Some innocently anticipate that Americans will adapt to their values and behaviors. Others avoid interacting with Americans or withdraw into the expatriate community to find comfort and relief from the complexity of their lives with Americans. Such behaviors, if they continue beyond a temporary reaction to the stress of cultural adaptation, can hold back students from experiencing a fuller richer experience during their stay in the United States.

Some students arrive in the United States with no real motivation to adapt to a social life with Americans. They genuinely prefer to live and socialize with other international students and concentrate on their academic challenges. Other students, however, arrive hoping to befriend Americans, experience a new culture, expand their understanding of people and the world, and gain a greater cultural awareness, only to find themselves seeking refuge with compatriots or avoiding interactions with Americans because of difficulties they encounter.

It is important to understand and recognize these impeding behaviors so that international students who genuinely want to gain deeper access into the culture and life in the United States can do so. Hopefully the narratives in Chapters 9 and 10 will bring about a deeper understanding for American and international student readers about why some students withdraw, avoid, complain, and react with an ethnocentric impulse. Such an understanding will hopefully be used to draw discouraged international students into the American community where they can establish friendships and deepen their awareness of American culture.

Although international students need to make efforts to adapt, all responsibility for cultural adaptation should not be up to the international student. The university community needs to be sincere in welcoming all international students, and should provide a positive, helpful community. Many universities and colleges do this through an orientation of the international affairs office and through foreign student advisors, international student associations, religious organizations, intramural sports programs, language institute programs, professors who specialize in cross-cultural communication and studies, and college and department clubs and activities that involve and reach out to international students.

Theme Four: Strategies and Successful Adaptation

The fourth theme (Part 5, Chapters 11–14) is about strategies that seem to be quite useful to international students as they adapt to their new lives in the United States. As discussed earlier, international students in our study used a number of strategies to adapt to life and university culture in the United States, including the use of humor, optimism, observation and behavior-matching, reflection on behavior, and seeking support within the American university community.

These diverse set of strategies appear to be quite useful, and I highly recommend international students explore their use. In addition, I recommend other potentially useful strategies, as discussed by others. Weaver (2000b), for example, provides several ways to reduce the strong feelings associated with culture shock (such as sadness, anxiety, homesickness, helplessness, confusion, and self-doubt). One way is to transfer potent reminders from home, such as photographs and favorite CDs. Other ways are to share feelings with others who understand the process of adaptation, write long letters to friends or family who have experienced cultural adaptation, and develop stress-control techniques, such as relaxing and minimizing the number of changes in a short period of time.

Weaver also suggests that students learn something about the new culture before leaving home. This is what a Japanese student did, as illustrated in the narrative, *Next Stop: USA* (Chapter 2). She prepared to study and live in the United States by studying at a language institute with American instructors, writing in an English diary, and watching American films and TV shows and then talking about them with her sister and a friend. Weaver also advises sojourners to study history, geography, food, religion, and other subjects that can provide background knowledge to the place the person will be living.

Theme Five: Readapting to the Home Culture and Reflecting on Living Abroad

The fifth theme (Part 6, Chapters 15–16) is on readjusting to the home culture and reflections on living abroad. This theme is included because many international students are stunned at how difficult it is for them to readapt to their home culture. Some are also astonished at how much they have gained from their overseas experience. Many come to realize how valuable their experience has been only after returning home.

Problems on returning home are closely connected to what Smith (1996) and Storti (1996) term *reverse culture shock*. Storti points out that this process of reentry usually begins with a honeymoon phase in which "home is close to perfect, very much what you imagined coming home would be like" (p. 49). Returning students visit old friends, enjoy home cooking and eat their favorite foods, and enjoy many of the things that they missed.

However, the honeymoon ends quickly, and reverse culture shock develops. The dislikes suddenly become more noticeable, and everything about the overseas experience is remembered in an idealistic way. The problems are forgotten and the good ties are remembered. Some individuals become judgmental, claiming that many parts of the home culture don't measure up to the way things are done in the United States. Students sometimes lose the ability to be objective and patient and tend to exhibit a variety of negative feelings, such as anger, depression, or anxiety, and often want to return to life overseas (Storti, 1996).

Weaver (2000a) points out that in some ways reentry shock is worse than the culture shock students experienced when they were adapting to the university and local community culture in the United States. Individuals in the host country expect international students to make mistakes and to be different. However, at home everyone expects the returning student to fit in quickly. Family and friends may not be especially tolerant of mistakes and may have little empathy for the difficulties of readapting to the culture.

In addition, for students who come from high-context cultures (many African, Asian, and Latino countries), reentry is further complicated by the fact that the returnee has less privacy than he or she has become accustomed to. Returning to a culture that values close contact and personal interaction, the returning student cannot gain privacy easily. Seeking ways to be alone or simply sleeping a lot could be "viewed as bizarre" (Weaver, 2000a, p. 224).

As in the narratives in Chapter 15 show, one thing that complicates the lives of some international students is that they have changed their personal values. This is especially a problem for those students who have spent considerable time in the United States or have been highly influenced by American culture. For example, several women returnees from Japan who took jobs in traditional Japanese corporations have told me that the hardest part of readjusting has been accepting a subordinate role in the workplace. Despite their excellent language abilities and education, they suddenly had to serve tea, run errands, and do menial tasks because they were women and new to the corporation. Their attitude about the role of women had changed, and they were faced with having to work in a Japanese setting that did not appreciate their values. A narrative in Chapter 15 by a single female Korean returnee also shows how attitudes can change. Independent and still single, she explains how much she now dislikes personal questions about her marital status.

Weaver (2000a) discusses other reasons reentry can be difficult, especially for students who came from a culture where context and nonverbal cues are an especially important part of communication. After spending years in the United States, many students seem well-adapted to the low-context way of communicating. The international students have learned to pay attention to what is said and become less conscious of nonverbal messages (tone of voice, posture, facial expressions, special distance, eye contact, gestures). As Weaver states, "In the United States [a returnee's] verbal abilities are highly rewarded and reinforced while his nonverbal subtlety only leads to confusion" (2000a, p. 222).

Although most international students still maintain some awareness of nonverbal behavior during their low-context, face-to-face interactions, when they return home, they might interact with people from their home culture in ways that seem strange from the perspective of the returnee's family and friends. Weaver (2000a) provides an example of an African student who pulled away from his cousin's grip and backed away from those who were talking to him because he had been keeping an arm's length from Americans while studying in the United States. Family, friends, and even strangers reacted to such behavior as distant, cold, or standoffish.

Storti (1996) points out that as time goes by reentry shock and its associated problems gradually diminish. Most students get used to being home and reach a stage when they can focus on their life as it is now and not how it used to be. As time passes, perspective grows; students no longer want to go overseas again as soon as possible; and they disclose that certain things within their home culture are pleasant, and certain things about living abroad were not as perfect as they once imagined.

Returning home is not only about reentry problems; for many international students it is also about fulfilling goals and gaining a new awareness about themselves and the world around them. As highlighted in the narratives in Chapter 16, and discussed by Adler (1987), having experienced another culture and undergone a process of adaptation, returning students gain a unique self-awareness.

While they live in the United States and deal with culture shock, including the emotional reactions to it, international students are challenged to handle these emotions and to find the strength to live and study in a place that seems ambiguous, unsympathetic, and difficult, and that tests their values and perceived ways of doing things. Students also have to meet academic and language challenges; some have doubts about their abilities to academically succeed. To meet these challenges, students need to look inside themselves to find the strength to continue, and by doing so, they often find themselves stronger at the end.

A number of international students return home feeling enriched from their experience with Americans. There is a new dimension to their identity, one that is partly American, and they are aware of the changes within them. Many international students gain a deeper understanding of their own native culture as a result of having lived in the United States. For example, the narrative in Chapter 16 by a student from Kazakhstan shows how deep such cognizance can be through her comparison of American culture with her native culture of Kazakhstan. Having opportunities to reflect on their culturally influenced lives provides international students with a fresh perspective of the values and behavior in their home cultures.

These five cultural adaption themes, and the narratives that accompany them throughout this book, are meant to provide readers with a framework for understanding the challenges facing international students.

PART 1
REFLECTIVE QUESTIONS

1. Begley (2006) defines *ethnocentrism* as "a bias leading people to judge another culture's habits and practices as right and wrong, good or bad according to their own cultural attitudes, beliefs, and values" (p. 389). How can ethnocentrism impede cultural adaptation?

2. Which challenges do you think are the most difficult for international students? Why?

3. The basic process of cultural adaptation includes five phases: (1) getting ready to leave, (2) initial experiences, (3) increasing interaction, (4) culture shock, and (5) adaptation. We have discovered that not all international students go through these phases in a linear order. Instead, for some, the process is more recursive with students going from one phase to another, after which they regress back to a previous phase. Why do you think this happens?

4. This book includes five themes (Parts 2–6). What are these five themes? Which theme strikes you as being the most interesting? Why?

The Basic Phases of Cultural Adaptation

The theme of Part 2 is on the basic phases of cultural adaptation that most international students go through. These phases include: (1) getting ready to leave, (2) initial experiences, (3) increasing interaction, (4) culture shock, and (5) adaptation. These phases are illustrated in Chapters 2–6 through spoken or written narratives by international students or Americans who interact with them or have observed their interactions with others.

CHAPTER 2

Phase One: Preparing to Leave

This chapter focuses on the thoughts and feelings of students who are preparing to leave their home countries to study in the United States.

Next Stop: USA — A Student from Japan Prepares to Study Abroad

The first narrative shows how a Japanese student decides to do what Begley (2006) sees as being an important adaptation strategy, that of anticipating and preparing to meet the challenges of living abroad.

I studied English in Japan for many years, but I was so worried about coming to the United States! Could I understand American English in real communication? Could I understand lecture? I worried a lot. So, I decided to prepare.

First, I studied English intensively for one year in Japan. I took oral communication class and writing class at a language institute. My teachers—all American. That helped me a lot, I think, to understand Americans' natural speech.

On weekends I recorded and watched American TV dramas, movies, comedy shows, and news. I watched some of these programs with my older sister, who studied English in America, and my friend who wanted to go to America too. We watched programs without Japanese subtitles. Then we talked about the show. Then, we watched the show with subtitles to see if we understood. I also wrote down new vocabulary in my notebook and looked them up in my computer dictionary or asked my American teacher. This helped me to understand spoken English on television, and my vocabulary became larger.

I also used Internet chat room to have conversation with Americans and people from other countries. I asked American and Asian university students questions about their life in United States and their courses—for example, what they study and how hard it is. I had fun, too! Sometimes we talked about traveling to interesting places in the U.S. or about good movies.

Sometimes I used Google to search for information about American life. I sometimes, how do I say, searched without a reason. I just typed in something like *conversation eating dinner American home*. I learned a lot this way about American life. For example, I learned about American dinner invitations and conversation topics at a dinner table.

The hardest thing for me is writing papers in English. I was afraid about writing. So, I decided to keep diary. I used to keep diary in Japanese. So, I decided to write every day in my English diary. At first it was so hard. I only wrote few sentences, sometimes just words. But, after few months, I can write a lot. I can now think in English. Some of my Asian friends struggle to write and have to translate a lot.

I am very happy I prepared to come to United States. I have good grades, and I can communicate with Americans. But, it wasn't so easy at first. I had some problems. But, I have less problems maybe, I think, because I prepared. ■

Anticipating Paradise—A Student from Niger Has Lofty Expectations

The second narrative illustrates the kinds of expectations that some international students have about living in the United States. As this student's narrative illustrates, some students might have an overly idealistic perception about what life is going to be like.

Before I came to America I thought that everything would be easy for me. You know, I was thinking that life would be like paradise. I would have my government scholarship to pay my tuition and living expenses, and I thought it would be easy to get a job, to buy a car. My idea of paradise is that things like money would be available and that life would be good in general, just like you see in a movie, you know. When I saw American movies, I thought that these people are living in a paradise. It gave me the feeling that living in America is easy because it is easy to get a job, make money, and everything is cheaper and life is wonderful.

I thought that life would not be as tough as in my country. I thought the media I saw in Niger was representative of America. It makes life in Africa look harder comparatively.

But, in reality life is not easier. You simply have different problems. It is easier to make money. I got a job at the university cafeteria and another job at the African Studies library. I can save money and send it to my family in Africa. And, I bought a used car. But, the social aspect of life is missing and everything has become about money. Having riches is nothing if you are not happy.

Nobody told me that when I come here, I will be lonely and have hectic times. Nobody told me I will be depressed and miss Africa and miss my family so much. I call them often.

So, really, America is not a paradise like I thought. I had the paradise idea, but now I realize I was mistaken. ∎

Sad Farewell—A Student from Indonesia Leaves His Extended Family

For some international students leaving home and family and friends is very difficult to do. The next narrative illustrates how sad it is for a student from Indonesia to say goodbye to his family. This student won a scholarship from the Fulbright Foundation to study for a master's degree in the United States, and he knew he would be away from Indonesia for two years.

I grew up in a big family in a small town in central Java. My family consists of eight children, and I am the third son. My father was an elementary school's teacher and my mother just a housewife. My family just a simple and humble family, but we really enjoy our brotherhood. We share everything together. When I was a little boy, I always slept in one bed with two or three of my brothers. We eat in one big plate together.

I never been lonely. But, when the time came and I must go to America to study, I can say that it was the worst moment in my life. I feel very lonely and sad. I wanted to stay in Java in my heart, but I cannot say anything.

The night before my departure, all people in my neighborhood gathered in my house to say goodbye to me and we eat together as a farewell party. Everyone had a good time. They laugh and eat. I also laugh, but in my heart I cry.

The next day, all my family, my aunt, my cousins, all of them 20 people came to the bus station to say goodbye to me. At that time I hoped the bus is late so I could spend the time longer with all my beloved family.

When the bus came, that's the time for me to leave my all-beloved family. I hugged each of them and they give me their last words to me. My father said, "This is the best way for you to lift up the name of our family and don't worry about your brothers. I still able to afford them." My mother just said, "Don't leave the God behind." I could not say anything. I just tried to be strong man and smile to everyone. I asked my two brothers to study hard and not worry about money. "I will send you money from America every month," I said, although I didn't know how will my life in America be. I just wanted them not to worry about me.

When the bus moved, I wave my hand to them, and I still saw my sister wipe her tears from her cheek. That time I didn't want to leave my family. I also feel that I run away from my responsibility to my brothers and family. I could only sit on the bus and try not to cry. ■

CHAPTER 3

Phase Two: Initial Experiences

This chapter focuses on initial experiences that international students, and in one case an American student's Chinese mother-in-law, have had in their new cultural setting. This set of narratives shows a variety of experiences and reactions to the new culture—elation, gratitude, fear, frustration, and confusion.

Bedazzled—A Student from South Korea Is Quickly Smitten with America

The first narrative is a very positive reaction to the new culture. The Korean student who composed this narrative reflects back on her first days in the United States, and she expresses a variety of positive emotions—excitement, euphoria, optimism, and curiosity, emotions that Adler (1975) and Oberg (1960) highlight as often being a part of the initial experience of moving to a new culture.

> I came to the United States with fantasies and hopes which shaped my conceptions toward American people and culture in a dreamy way. My images as to Americans and culture were colored by TV, movies, magazines,

and music. Looking back, I cannot help laughing at my ignorance and naïveté. At the beginning of my stay in America, I kept thirsting for these fantasies to be true. I felt that the whole new wonderful world would open right in front of me.

Wherever I went, people greeted me even though they were strangers. Their enthusiastic greetings, "Hello! How are you?!" enabled me to open up to American culture easily and quickly. I wrote letters to my parents and friends back home about what a wonderful time I was having in the United States. I also took many pictures of roads, houses, landscapes, and smiling faces. I hoped to capture and share every single beautiful aspect of America in photographs so that I could show them to friends and family back home.

I was happy to live in a dorm at this small college in Tennessee to get acquainted with American people and culture as fast as I could. For the first few months, I tried to avoid meeting Korean students because I wanted to make the most of my stay in America. Since I felt Americans were so nice and friendly to me, I thought I could make a lot of American friends. It seemed to me that they were willing to be close and to give me the help I needed. Just speaking English with American people in my daily life made me feel so thrilled because in Korea it was hard for me to find someone I could practice English with.

I was so happy to get up in the morning. Usually I woke up at six o'clock every day because of my excitement. I spoke to a lot of American students in the dorm, and I intentionally went down to the lounge to watch TV and to meet more Americans. I laughed and enjoyed every moment. Nothing was likely to overshadow my happiness! ■

Unforgettable Ride—A Student from Pakistan Is Scared Stiff on the New York Subway

As with the happy Korean student in Tennessee, the student in the next narrative arrived in the United States with a playful, curious outlook. This adventurous young student from Pakistan had arrived in New York City only two days earlier to begin her studies at Columbia University, and being adventurous, she decided to take a late-night subway downtown to visit her friend. Little did she know that her lighthearted mood would be dashed by a terrifying subway ride.

"I'm finally on my own! Yay!!!" I said these exact words many times during the first two days in New York. I felt free as a bird. Happy to be out in the world and in New York City. I had moved into my dorm before other new students and explored the campus and a little of the Upper West Side on my own. I looked at grand cathedrals, and I watched people from so many different races and colors walk up and down the street. I sipped coffee at a sidewalk café. I wandered from shop to shop, buying fruits, pastries, and things I needed. It felt good to be there! I quickly fell in love with the city!

But, after spending two days by myself, I began to feel a little lonely. So, I decided to visit my friend from Pakistan on the Lower East Side. I called her, and she was happy to hear from me. Although it was already quite late, we both wanted to meet. So, I agreed to take a taxi to her apartment and to spend the night there.

"My first New York adventure," I thought. "It shouldn't be hard to take a taxi to her apartment." But, when I stood on Broadway, I couldn't find a taxi. And when I did see one, I could not get the driver to stop.

It was already close to ten, and I started to feel a little scared being on the street so late at night by myself. So, I thought, "There is a subway station right over there. I'll take the subway. Part of the adventure!" But, as I walked down the subway entrance steps, my adventurous feeling began to change. "What is that awful smell?"

I bought my token and studied my subway map again. "Yes. This is the correct train," I thought. I looked around the platform. I was alone, and I started to feel a little worried. "Have I made a mistake? What am I doing? I am alone in a strange city on a New York City subway platform at night. Maybe I should go back to my dorm room." But, as I turned to go back, I heard the screech of the subway coming closer to the station.

"So far, so good!" I looked around. The compartment was relatively clean. I tried not to stare at anyone. But, I did glance at the riders through the corner of my eye. I felt relieved to see three young well-dressed women sitting near me. A young couple giggled in a corner. An old man looked dirty and tired. A man in a baseball cap read a newspaper. Then, I suddenly saw a big man looking at me. "Oh no! Stay calm." I took out my book and started to read.

At the next stop the big man got off the subway. Then, all of a sudden three boys, maybe teenagers, with plastic covering over their faces ran into our compartment, followed by the police! The subway door closed, and we were trapped as the police ran after them.

"Stop! Freeze!" I heard a policeman yell. He had a gun aimed at one of the boys. I abruptly comprehended and was absolutely petrified! I could hear the gasps of other passengers and felt my whole body growing weak. At this wretched moment, all I could think was going back to my safe and secure home in Pakistan.

It ended. The boys surrendered. The police assured us that the situation was under control. I could still feel my legs shaking. I must have appeared to be very frightened as one of the policeman asked me if I was alright. I told him I just arrived in New York and did not know my way around in what must have been a panic-like voice. He offered to escort me to my friend's apartment.

My friend opened the door to her apartment to welcome me. She was, needless to say, very surprised to see me with a policeman. ■

Although some students begin their stay in the United States with a playful, curious, and excited attitude about being in a new culture, as the previous narrative shows, dealing with the dark sides of their new surroundings is one of many challenges.

My Hand's Up, and It's My Turn! — A Student from Britain Feels Ignored in Class

Another challenge for many international students is learning to interact in American English. The next narrative takes us into the classroom where many of the cultural rules for interaction are unique to American university culture. This short narrative illustrates that something as simple as raising a hand to answer a question does not necessarily have the same meaning across cultures.

The narrative also raises an important subject—that of *ethnocentrism*. As DeCapua and Wintergerst define it, "ethnocentrism is the belief in the intrinsic superiority of one's own culture, language, and/or ethnic group . . . . It is a highly subjective, personal, emotional, and (usually) subconscious way of valuing one's own culture above other cultures" (2004, p. 63). The British student is open to understanding and adapting to American classroom behavior and does so remarkably well in time.

However, at this early point in his adaptation, he still conjectures that the best way for teachers to call on students is the British way.

I am British, and I am in United States to study as a graduate student. I am an enthusiastic student, and want to participate in the classroom. During my first month here, I have been rather frustrated to find myself sitting in class with my hand permanently up. Not that I mind signaling my desire to share yet another 10-cent nugget, but the experience of being repeatedly ignored is annoying. It has seemed like the teachers do not see that it is my turn to speak.

However, I believe I now understand why the instructors do not call on me. In Britain, teachers, like bartenders, are morally obliged to remember who is next. This way everyone has a chance to contribute to the discussion. But, here the teacher seems to randomly acknowledge a student to answer or ask a question. Or, more likely, as I am beginning to recognize in some of my smaller seminar classes, only those students who raise their hand and shout out at the appropriate, or even inappropriate, moment manage to get a word in edgewise.

If I am correct, I have to change the way I attempt to contribute to our seminar discussions. But, I am not sure that I can change my British way of waiting for the teacher to call on me. It just seems to be a more polite and fair way to conduct a proper class. ∎

Huh? What? Excuse Me?—
A Student from Taiwan Struggles
to Comprehend

The next narrative describes a different kind of initial experience, one that reveals a student's unease about her English comprehension abilities and capability to live and study in the United States.

After flying, I step on ground of this famous country of freedom. I was so excited to be here! I felt so happy to be in United States!

But, my happiness, it only stay short time. I have big problem. I can't understand what people say to me—Americans and international student. I guess I have problem to understand accent of everyone!

I hoped professors, though, will speak more clearly. But, yesterday I met one professor, and I am in trouble. I really had hard time to understand her. She talk so quickly! When she asked me question, I can only say, "Huh? What? Excuse me?"

Everyone is so nice. They repeat what they say in different way and speak slow. But, many times I can't understand, just pretend. I feel so embarrass. My poor listening ability.

All the time I smile. I smile and smile! My new friends say, "You look so friendly. You always smile." But really I am not smile on inside. Will I ever understand? Is my English good enough? ■

Misunderstanding on Taylor Street—A Mother-in-Law from China Learns about Morning Exercise and the Police

The next narrative is different as it is not about an international student. Rather, it is about an American graduate student's Chinese mother-in-law who had just arrived from China. The kind of initial experience she had will be evident from the story. More important, it illustrates the concept of *perceptual relativity* (J.M. Bennett, 1998; Singer, 1998) where "people behave as they do because of ways in which they perceive the external world" (Singer, 1998, p. 97). In this narrative, the Chinese mother-in-law and her American neighbors had very different perceptions about when, where, and what kind of exercise is appropriate.

"Who are these people, and what do they want?" my mother-in-law must have been thinking when she was suddenly approached by several men holding flashlights and speaking excitedly in a strange language. My mother-in-law, who came here from Beijing only two weeks ago, was doing her normal exercise routine in the school yard across the street, an hour before sunrise. The men holding flashlights were policemen, and the "strange language" was our local variety of English.

My mother-in-law is one of the many millions of Chinese who consider it an essential part of every day to rise early, while the air is cleanest and the world most at peace, to go through the ancient set of movements known as *t'ai chi chu'an*. Unfortunately for my mother-in-law, on this particular morning she used a sword in her exercises. Although this sword is collapsible and quite blunt, I'm sure it was not obvious to the neighbor or passerby who called the police.

After my flustered translations and explanations, and a fairly civilized handling of the affair, the police understood what had happened. However, it was unfortunate that they found it necessary to use force to *disarm* my elderly mother-in-law. Oh! My poor mother-in-law! Her unique problems of adjusting to a new culture! ■

CHAPTER 4

Phase Three: Increasing Interaction and Challenges

As international students continue to have more and more cultural encounters, some gradually become overwhelmed with their daily interactions. However, it is not just the big surprises, such as a scary encounter on a subway, that overwhelms them. Rather, many students start to feel inundated by the multitude of small, everyday interactions, many of which are beyond the students' awareness. These interactions not only include nonverbal behavior but also social-cultural behavior. The narratives in this chapter reveal how cultural cues or signals include things like when to stop taking a shower, when to remove your shoes, how to take a phone message, how to convince a crude roommate not to eat your food, and how to keep interpersonal harmony.

When international students interact in their native cultures, cultural cues make them feel comfortable because they are automatic and natural. However, when they arrive in the United States and attempt to interact in a new social setting, the cues change. Further, most international students do not realize the cause of their discomfort is that they learned their "own kinesic, proxemic, and chronemic cues simply by growing up in (their) own culture" (Weaver, 2000b, p. 179).

Living with an American Family— A Student from Japan Recognizes Cultural Cues and Changes His Habits

The first narrative illustrates how a Japanese student living with a host family learned new cultural cues or indicators to behave in culturally appropriate ways. He learned to accept second helpings at the dinner table, as well as the cues indicating another family member wants to use the bathroom (e.g., knocking on the door and shouting, "Hurry up!"). He also was able to resolve problems, such as not feeling comfortable wearing shoes in the house.

I lived with an American family in suburban New Jersey when I was a student at a language institute. That was eight years ago, before I studied for my undergraduate and now graduate degree, but it seems like yesterday. The family included a husband, his wife who is a homemaker, and two daughters, ages fifteen and twelve then. It was a wonderful experience for me to use everyday English with Americans, and I learned to do things in an American way. But, I remember it wasn't so easy sometimes.

Of course I already knew about not taking off my shoes in the house before I came to the United States. So, when I started to live with the American family, I did the same thing. But, my feet felt tired all the time from wearing shoes. I didn't realize how much Japanese houses are comfortable because we take our shoes off at the entrance hall. So, I really wanted to take them off. I mentioned this to Heather, the youngest daughter, and she suggested, "Why not wear slippers?" That was the solution. In a Japanese house we sometimes wear slippers, and some Americans do, too. My feet felt much better.

I ate meals with the family in the evening. Everyone gathered at the table in the dining room at 6:30. It was a family rule. I felt like I was member of the family. I liked that very much. But, it took me a long time before I can do the same, like the family. I remember when I first lived there I became thinner and thinner. This is because I didn't eat much even if hungry. In Japan when someone offers you something, like more food, you are polite and say "no thank you" until the person offers a few times or insists. So when my American mother asked me, "More meat? More potato? More milk?" I always said, "No, thank you." Then she didn't ask again. She simply said, "Help yourself if you're hungry."

I understood what she meant, but I felt strange to say "yes" when she offered, and I felt even more strange to help myself. But, I realized I should do the same as Americans. So, a few days later when my American mother asked me if I want more chicken, I said, "Yes, please." I wasn't even hungry, but I was very happy. It was so easy. I felt like I changed that day. I became like Americans.

I had to change a lot of habits when I lived with the family. One habit in Japan was taking a long hot shower and bath. So, when I lived with my American family, I took a long shower every morning. But, I didn't know that other family members waited for me to finish and that I caused problems for them. No one said anything to me for about a week. Then, one morning Emily knocked hard on the door and yelled, "Hurry up! I want to take a shower!" I was so shocked. I hurried and left the bathroom without finishing my shower or shave. That evening, Emily started suddenly to complain. She complained that she had to wait for me to finish taking a shower in the morning, the water was cold, and she had to rush to go to school.

I was embarrassed. I wondered how I could take a shower in less time and use less hot water. So, I tried a plan. The first thing I did was to wait to take a shower until the other family members did. I also counted how much time each person took in taking a shower, which turned out to be four to seven minutes. Then, I tried to take a shower in ten minutes, which was the minimum time as I could. This worked. I almost forgot about the Japanese way of taking a bath, and I learned to take a fast American shower like my American family. ■

Telephone Misconnections— An American Host and a Student from Hong Kong Realize Cultural Barriers to Taking Phone Messages

The next narrative is from the perspective of a home-stay mother who learned she was not as sensitive to other cultural behavior as she had thought and that a cultural cue for *not* taking a phone message in Hong Kong can be the nature of the call itself.

I decided to be a host to an international student from Hong Kong. I wanted to provide a comfortable home where this student could experience a typical American family. I wanted to make this experience one where the student would be able to gain a new cultural understanding and appreciation for American culture, at least the culture that I represent.

However, in my relationship with this young student, Lily, I created an episode that was painful for both of us. The difficulty centered around answering the telephone and taking messages. I fully realize that talking on the phone in a foreign language is much more difficult than face-to-face contact. One reason is because there are no contextual and nonverbal clues to rely on for understanding or making oneself understood.

I have been a host mother for a number of students, and most constantly express their anxiety about phone conversations and find all kinds of ways to avoid answering the phone. But, after several months, Lily had become accustomed to chatting at length with her friends on the phone in English and Cantonese, and I had given her an explicit protocol for taking phone messages in my absence. That is why I became increasingly irritated at being told that "someone called."

"Who was it?"

"A woman."

"What was her name?"

"She didn't tell me."

"Did you ask her?"

"No."

"Lily, always ask. Ask who is calling before you even say that I'm not here. That way they don't have a chance to hang up before you find out."

"Sometimes they say it, but I don't understand because I don't know so many American names."

"I know."

"Okay. So, just take your time, ask, and write it down. Then when you say that I'm not here, the person can leave a message or number so I can call them back."

"Okay."

Simple. The same instructions I had given my own children when they reached an age where they were allowed to answer the phone. Still, another day would come and I'd find a note on the kitchen table: "A woman called at 2:30." Again the conversation about taking messages. Lily was close to tears. I was out of patience. "What is so hard about this?"

"I don't know if a business call or a friend."

"What difference does that make?"

Lily started to cry and her English started to regress, "I don't think you want I be rude your friends."

"Ohhh! Then how do you answer the phone in Hong Kong?"

"When I was secretary, I ask, 'Who may I say is calling?'"

"How about the phone at home?"

"Calls if not for me, can call back. If not my friend is not my business. Maybe phone call is for my sister, not me. Person will become angry and complain if I rude to them."

"Ahhh," I later thought to myself. "It's not appropriate to ask for information about someone's personal calls!" I soon realized this is why Lily was having such a problem taking messages. She didn't want to be rude to callers by asking for a name and message. How odd that it took us weeks to straighten this out. What I was asking Lily to do was a familiar routine, but it was only appropriate for business calls for her. Calls from friends are a private matter. That one missing cross-cultural link had kept us from connecting and had created increasing unnecessary tension. After a careful and complete discussion of telephone protocols in *both* cultures, Lily started presenting me with complete and accurate messages, and I discontinued my "rude" behavior toward her callers:

"Lily, someone called you today."

"Oh, okay, they will call back. You got call from your friend Karen about breakfast on Saturday. If you want to cancel, you can call her. But if you not call, she will see you there at nine o'clock." ■

The Innocent Lie— A Japanese Student's Lie to Preserve Harmony Backfires with a Plain-Talking American

The next narrative shows how values and related behavior can create misunderstanding. This student discovered that her values, which allow telling a lie to maintain harmony, resulted in creating disharmony.

I was living in San Francisco where I studied English. My new life was great. I had many friends from different countries. Many Americans lived in a residential hotel where I was staying, so I could communicate with people in English. I was happy hanging around with my new friends.

One of my new friends, an American guy in the hotel, asked me to go out on New Year's Eve. I said yes, even though I didn't know him well. I had no plan at the time and didn't want to spend New Year's Eve alone. But a few days later my friends from school invited me to their party. I felt guilty but I really wanted to go to my friends' party, so I apologized to him and told him that I could not go out with him because I was invited to my friends' party. He agreeably understood me and said, "Have a good time!" I went to the party and enjoyed it very much.

A couple days later I met him at the hotel lobby. He asked me whether I had fun at the party. I still felt guilty, so I lied to him. I said I didn't have a good time at the party and I regretted that I didn't go out with him.

Suddenly, "Damn it!" he shouted at me. "You chose to go to the party and didn't have fun?! What about me? I didn't agree to break our date to hear that!"

I was shocked that I actually heard that. I was expecting him to say, "Oh, I'm sorry. See, I told you that you should come with me," or things like that. I was surprised by the unexpected reaction.

I criticized the party because that was the polite way in my culture. I told him a lie because I wanted to make him feel better. But his way was different. He would have been satisfied by hearing the truth that I had a good time at the party.

I still don't know if that was a cross-cultural miscommunication. My life in the United States is a repetition of such events. Sometimes I see the contrast to my culture and understand the difference, but sometimes I don't know whether it is caused by cultural misunderstanding or personal differences or both. I do know that my life here is complex! ■

Life with a Crude American— A Student from Costa Rica Copes with a Tactless Roommate

The next narrative shows a different aspect of adjustment, that of conflict due both to cultural and personality problems. A student from Costa Rica decided to share a university apartment with an American student. However, the American turned out to be disreputable, and the life of the Costa Rican student became perplexing and difficult.

When I was still in Costa Rica, I applied to live in one of the on-campus apartments. As I needed to watch my spending, I signed up to share an apartment with another student, and I requested American. When I arrived at the university and checked into the apartment, I met my roommate, and I felt happy because he seemed to be a nice and organized person.

One of the first things my roommate did was to set "the rules of the game." He said that in order for us to get along with each other we should be very sincere and have a lot of communication. "If you have a problem, or if there is something that I do that bothers you," he said, "you should let me know so that we can work it out." I thought that it was pretty reasonable and beneficial for both of us since we were going to spend an academic year living in the same place.

One of the rules we established was to clean up after ourselves. He also said that if it was okay with me, we should share our food. But, I didn't agree. I thought it was better for me to have my own food. He said that this would be fine.

It did not take long to notice that my roommate was eating all my food! I would go grocery shopping, and as soon as I got back, he would start eating the food I had just bought. It was uncomfortable for me because I did not touch his groceries. What disturbed me the most was the way he treated my food. I would come home to find a can of beans in the trash with half of its content still in the can, or I might find him having a meal and eating two or three of my things all at the same time. When I mentioned our agreement to him, he simply laughed and said, "Rules are made to be broken! Don't worry about it. Have some of my food."

Other things I found that I didn't like about my roommate were some of his habits. He never made his bed, and he had a pile of dirty clothes on the floor. This pile was there for more than six months! In addition to this, he never washed the dirty dishes or pots and pans. He just set them in the sink. I didn't want to wash them for him, but what really bothered me was that whenever I needed something to cook with, I would have to wash it. He also never vacuumed or cleaned anything. I remember that he used to say things like, "Oh, I think we need to clean the toilet," but he wouldn't clean it. We had cleaning products that I had bought, but he never attempted to use them. He also never bought any other basic supplies—paper napkins, bathroom tissue, soap. I always had to provide these things.

When the academic year came to an end and we had to clean up the apartment before we moved out, my roommate gathered his stuff and left the day before me. I had to clean the entire apartment myself or we would have to pay a fine. On top of that, he took my coffeemaker with him! I didn't report this because I didn't want to have any problems since it was the end of the year, and I had other important issues to think about. However, I still wonder what my roommate's reaction would have been if I had taken his microwave "by mistake," as he would probably say if I ran into him on campus! ■

Tongue-Tied—A Student from Taiwan Struggles to Overcome Her Fear of Using English in Front of Her American Classmates

The next narrative reminds us that some students not only are challenged with cultural adaptation, they also face anxieties about using English. In the two narrative segments, a student describes her battle against a high level of anxiety about speaking English in front of her American classmates and professor. Although her English is very advanced, she worries incessantly about expressing her ideas in class. Arnold and Brown (1999), Ohata (2004), Scovel (1978), and Young (1999) have written about second language learning and anxiety, emphasizing the link between anxiety and second language performance. The narrative speaks to this link.

*A*fter the third class:

I looked around the classroom on the first day, and I counted fifteen students, and I could see only one other Asian student. The others, Americans. When I decided to come to this small college to complete my junior year as an exchange student from Taiwan, I thought it will be good chance for me to improve my English, especially speaking. But, now I worry a lot that American classmates cannot understand my Taiwanese English. It makes me nervous.

This class is not a lecture. It is a seminar, and the teacher, she said we are expected to prepare for every class and to participate during class discussion. So to prepare for the next two classes, I read through the reading materials very carefully and looked up every single word that I did not understand. Sometimes I reread the pages to make sure I understand the whole concept. But, even though I prepared and wanted to contribute during the discussion, somehow I was unable to do it. I could not even utter a word. After every class, like right now, I feel so upset. How can I study so hard but still not give any opinions in class? Why am I so nervous? The teacher must think I do not prepare.

After the tenth class:

Well, I still don't speak very much in class. It is hopeless. One reason is because every time I get some ideas, I am anxious about using correct English, so I tend to rehearse my lines in my mind first to make sure I use correct words and grammar. Whenever I am ready to raise my hand, I find the cruel fact that the subject of discussion has moved to the next one.

When I do speak, it is obvious that I am nervous, and one thing that bothers me a lot is about my physical reaction to nervousness. Whenever I speak in the class, I tend to blush quite easily. My classmates told me that I sometimes even have some rash on my neck. I feel embarrassed when others can see I am nervous. So, this makes me more anxious about speaking. I don't understand why I am so afraid to speak English. My classmates are all very nice. When I do speak up in class, the professor always gives me a friendly smile to ease my tension. I guess I will have to try harder. ■

CHAPTER 5

Phase Four: Culture Shock

Most international students arrive in the United States ready to face environmental, linguistic, academic, and social challenges. They are often surprised, however, at how difficult it is to adapt. The weather is colder than they predicted; the food is more problematic than they imagined; and using English in academics and their social lives is more challenging than they envisioned.

Many international students find adaptation difficult because their familiar ways of doing things vaporize and are replaced by a multitude of new ways to accomplish everyday, simple things. There are obvious differences, such as the American students who bring coffee, soft drinks, and food to class, or the fact that many Americans show physical affection in public places. But such easily observable behaviors are easy to understand. The problem for many international students is in adapting to the multitude of different behaviors that are not as obvious, such as how Americans greet, introduce, interrupt, take turns speaking, pass food at a dinner table, stand in line, open a gift, register for classes, and ask the teacher questions. Even more challenging are all the small micro-behaviors (Hall, 1998) found in nonverbal cues that tell people how to behave in certain situations, such as whether or not to pass an approaching person on a sidewalk on the left or right, or when and how long to look into a person's eyes during a conversation. These behaviors differ across cultures and are usually out of our awareness (Anderson & Wang, 2006; Hall, 1998; Morain, 1986). Such ongoing challenges saturate international students' daily lives and can become emotionally taxing and lead to culture shock.

Brown (2000), Kohls (1996), and Storti (1989) point out symptoms of culture shock, including anxiety, homesickness, helplessness, boredom, depression, fatigue, confusion, self-doubt, weeping, paranoia, and physical ailments. Culture shock can also lead to isolating behavior, as when students stay alone in their rooms, read and study excessively, avoid contact with Americans, and solely befriend people from their own homeland. Some students also have what Kohls (1996) calls "aggressive symptoms," including compulsive eating, obsessive drinking, exaggerated cleanliness, and hostility toward Americans.

This chapter offers two narratives that aim at a deeper understanding of how culture shock occurs. Each narrative shows the process through which the students went from being excited and happy to be in the United States to showing the symptoms of culture shock.

What's Happened to Roger?— An American Student Sees Behavioral Changes in Her Malaysian Boyfriend

The first narrative provides an observation of the changes that an American witnessed in her Malaysian boyfriend. These changes show how deeply culture shock can affect a student's behavior and attitude.

> I met Roger two years ago when a mutual friend introduced us. Before moving to the U.S. from Malaysia, Roger had been a personal physical fitness trainer. He had trained clients from around the world, had numerous certifications in the field, and loved his work. But, he wanted to further formalize his experience; so he came to the United States to study Physical Therapy. I taught

women strength training at the time and enjoyed meeting people from around the world. I was also a nontraditional student at the university.

As we have similar interests, Roger and I got along wonderfully from the start and became close friends. We frequented the movie theater, did aerobics, and went cycling, running, swimming, and dancing together. We listened to music and were surprised to find out we were both obsessed with the same genre—the '80s! One day as we were packing our suits for a swim, Roger exclaimed, "I can't believe two people who grew up on opposite sides of the world could have so much in common!"

Roger would cook his favorite ethnic dishes and show me how to eat with my fingers, as he had learned. He would talk to me about Kuala Lumpur, where he lived as a young adult, and Malacca, the historical coastal town where he was raised. He would go on and on about the food, the palm trees, the warm weather, and the beautiful beaches. I thought he was sharing his life with me. Now I know it was that and more. I didn't know it at the time, but Roger was leaving the exciting adventurous stage of his stay in the States. He was about to embark on a dark journey of doubt and depression; he was entering a stage of culture shock.

Roger started to complain about the snow-covered terrain, a freezing apartment that was poorly insulated, the food, and a grueling semester of classes. The climate alone was a sharp contrast to the hot and humid tropics he had left behind. Suddenly everyone was immature and incompetent, and everything about the U.S. and the university was inadequate. He reminisced about Malaysia and glorified every aspect of his homeland, while simultaneously criticizing everything in his hometown. He would dwell on the fact that he had been reduced to the status of a student, after working as a professional for over a decade. "What have I done? I had a good life. I think I really made a mistake."

Roger forced himself out of bed every day to attend his classes. Studying was a grueling chore. He lost his coping skills. On the weekends he slept all day. After studying for awhile, he would sleep more. He complained of feeling sore and achy all the time, and every other week he was convinced that he was getting the flu.

What happened to the motivated, focused, energetic man I had met four months earlier? What happened to the man who caught my heart by dancing around my apartment while playing music from the '80s?

Not knowing what the true cause of his change in personality and overall pessimism was, I began to resent Roger's incessant complaining. I took it very personally and believed that it was an indication that we weren't right for each other. After all, what's a girl to think when her boyfriend doesn't want to have coffee, see a movie, or simply take a walk? I tried talking to him about it. He assured me that I wasn't the reason for his angst. He could only identify it as stress. I was losing patience; I now had a boyfriend whose needs seemed to be overwhelming me.

At the time, I had no idea that Roger's depression was related to culture shock. It never crossed my mind because he had seemed so comfortable in his new environment when we first met. He was fluent in English, had made friends outside his own ethnicity, learned the driving laws and drove a car, and was managing straight A's in his classes. I was so naïve to think those were all easy adjustments for him to make. I was unaware of the amount of energy he had to exert every day to maintain the image he had created for himself. He made it look so easy. It was also naïve of me to think he was immune to the emotional and physical hardship of living in another country.

I now understand more about cultural adjustment and cultural shock, and I can more deeply appreciate Roger. He worked through his depression, and he regained some of the same flair and love for life. It is wonderful to see him happy again, and I have gained even more respect for this strong-willed man who loves to dance to the music of the 1980s. ■

Stranger at My Door—A Married Indian Student's Feeling of Isolation Sparks Her Wild Imagination

The second narrative illustrates how weeks of loneliness and isolation led to a critical incident that triggered severe symptoms of culture shock.

It was a crystal clear day when the flight attendant announced that we were passing the New York harbor and the Statue of Liberty. Looking down through the window, I said to myself, "How beautiful! Just the way I had read in the books." It was truly a sight I had dreamed once. The beauty of the view I saw was hard to describe.

Upon landing I saw my husband, who had come to the airport to pick me up, and from the airport, we drove to our new hometown near the university where he would study as graduate student and work as a research assistant, and I would begin to study the following semester as an undergraduate. As we drove, I observed the big buildings, wide highways, and curvy roads in the countryside where the houses were all spread out. The big farms were covered with corn and other crops. I had never seen such big farms in India. Compared to my urban life in India, this place looked very big, spacious, and clean.

Finally, we reached our new home. My husband had come a week earlier to find a place for us to live, and to my surprise it seemed to be very isolated, as it stood at the end of a driveway and some distance from other houses. There were six fully furnished rooms in our house, and there was a big yard with a fence. Never having seen a grassy yard like this in India, I almost started dancing with joy and excitement! Surrounded by the hills and evergreen trees, our house was far away from the city and was very quiet. I thought this quiet place would inspire me to study. There would not be anybody to interrupt me. I would have all my privacy, and I was very happy and felt very fortunate to be in the world's most beautiful place.

But, little by little I felt as if something was missing. At first I thought it was just my imagination, but as the days went by and things slowed down, I realized that there wasn't any excitement left. In my nice big house, I often was all by myself with nobody to see or talk to. I became very homesick and lonely.

I started to miss my life in India. I even missed the daily visits of the milkman, produce man, flower lady, and others who would show up at the door at any time. In India friends and relatives would visit often, too. I was becoming so homesick that I was losing my appetite, my ability to read and study, and my smile. Everything started to look pale, blunt, and dark. I felt as if I had been thrown from a busy, noisy place to a quite, pretty dungeon. I felt scared. Even a sudden breeze of air rustling the tree leaves would make my heart jump. Instead of being an inspiration, this new home was making me feel depressed and afraid.

When in this state of mind and emotion, I will never forget an incident that happened to me. It was a weekday afternoon, and I was all by myself in the house as my husband was at the university much of each day. All of a sudden I heard my doorbell ring. I jumped up! "Who could it be? I had not invited anybody, had I?" I assured myself that there wasn't anybody who I was expecting. My heart started to race. "Should I open the door or shouldn't I? What should I do? What if the stranger had a gun in his hand? What if he kidnapped me or raped me?" I didn't even know if the person was a man or a woman. "Oh...oh... no. I better pretend I'm not at home!" No matter what, I would not answer the door! Then, suddenly I decided to hide underneath my bed. There I went—running into my bedroom and crawling under my bed. I shook all over with fear as I heard the knocking grow louder and louder.

After a few minutes, it was dead quiet. It was so silent I could hear my racing heartbeat. I kept praying to God, "Please help me!" I knew that I was going to die and my husband would never see me again. I would never see my family in India again. I kept looking at the bedroom door from under the bed. "Oh no, what's that noise? Is that footsteps in the living room?" I could imagine a big man carrying a gun. Then, I heard a noise coming from outside. It sounded like a car door being closed. I could hear the start of an engine. "Okay. The person isn't inside the house; he's in his car and leaving," I thought.

I slowly crawled out from under the bed and to the bedroom window. On my hands and knees, I peeked out the window. The car was starting down my long driveway. "Oh no! It's our friend Peggy! Oh no! I ran down the stairs and out the door screaming, "P–e–g–g–y!" I waved my hands while running after the car, "Stop! I'm here! Come back!" Luckily Peggy saw me from her mirror and stopped.

It was an embarrassing moment; I was speechless. I didn't know how to explain what went into my mind, but Peggy quickly understood how scared I was. "Goodness! I am sorry for not calling before I came over. I thought I would bring you some of the fresh bread I just made."

After spending a good deal of time in this country and living in that house, I have become used to life here. I have made a lot of friends and have adapted to the quiet country life. I no longer get frightened when the doorbell rings, but I will always remember that scary incident when my over-zealous imagination went wild when I thought there was a stranger at my door. ∎

CHAPTER 6

Phase Five: Adaptation

Chapter 5 addressed the shock phase of cultural adaptation. For international students, culture shock typically results from constant cultural differences that take shape as a long series of small, everyday differences in interaction behavior and perceptual disparity. Such dissimilarity challenges, and even threatens, some international students' mostly unconscious understanding of the assumptions, values, and behavior that are a deep part of their upbringing. Coupled with academic, linguistics, and other challenges, international students, to various degrees, feel anxious, homesick, depressed, paranoid, helpless, fatigued, and more.

However, as international students confront such feelings, and reflect on their new lives, they start to accept the values and behaviors of people as simply different. Most realize that they need to change their own attitude and behavior in order to adapt. This process of adaptation is usually gradual for most students, as it takes time and some effort to orient themselves enough to be capable of inferring and using subtle cultural cues. For example, it took time and experience for the Japanese student in Chapter 4 to perceive what "help yourself" at the family dinner table actually means to Americans.

It is important to point out that not all sojourners, including international students, are able to fully or even partially adapt to a new culture. For example, and as discussed in Part 4, rather than interacting with Americans much of the day and learning from their experiences, some students withdraw into the expatriate community and socialize only with compatriots.

However, most international students gradually learn to adapt; as they increase their interactions and awareness, they elevate their ability to read and use cultural cues. Eventually, some international students even become bicultural. As Kohls (1996) points out, they will have an ability "to function in two cultures with confidence. [They] will even find a great many customs, ways of doing and saying things, and personal attitudes that [they] enjoy . . . and will definitely miss when [they] pack up and return home" (p. 98).

More Than Just Studying in America—A Student from Taiwan Overcomes Culture Shock

The first narrative is by a student who tells us about the challenges she faced in her academics and independent life while immersed in American culture, her strong reaction to the barrage of cultural differences that led to culture shock, and how she was able to adapt to her life in America.

I was ready to begin my new life in the United States, and I decided to live in a neighborhood without any Taiwanese. I had agreed with my sister that if I want to improve my English, I should keep some distance from the Taiwanese community. She told me, "Taiwanese students only hang out with their compatriots from Taiwan, and you will miss chances to speak a lot of English. They help you a lot, but they will also make it difficult to really experience the United States from the American perspective."

I could see right from the beginning that my sister was right. The Taiwanese Association met me at the airport, showed me how to shop for food, and helped me open a checking account. A group of Taiwanese students also let me stay with them the first few nights and even asked me to stay as a renter. I thought about doing this. But most of the day I didn't speak English.

So, I told them tactfully that I preferred to live in a bigger apartment. I then contacted an apartment manager who had an apartment that was some distance away from the Taiwanese community. I thought that was the first step in being independent.

But, being independent was not so easy. I had to apply for a telephone, for example, and that experience was very unpleasant. I walked around for 30 minutes in 92 degree temperatures to find a public phone to call the telephone company. The employee who took my call seemed very rude and impatient. She asked me questions comprised of terms such as *one-touch tone, unlimited calling,* and *caller ID,* which were Greek to me then. When I kept asking her to explain those terms to me, she lost her patience and told me, "Find someone who can speak English to talk with me." I was so frustrated that I couldn't resist thinking that Taiwanese are famous for hospitality. We treat foreigners with much consideration because we understand the uneasiness when people just come to a new environment.

I walked back to my apartment, and after taking a rest, I started to do self-counseling. It took awhile to convince myself that it was not my fault, and the rude attitude was just that individual. I told myself not to give up. Then, I called the company again. I was lucky this time. A nice employee helped me out. The phone was installed two days later, and I felt good. I felt independent, and I was doing everything in English.

Things changed quickly when school began. I found studying in the U.S. different from in Taiwan. I didn't know how to give presentations, participate in class discussion, or write academic papers in English. I never had those experiences in Taiwan. When I was confronted with a lot of reading and homework, invisible stress fogged me. The uncertainty of how to meet the professors' expectations made me very nervous. I had to take medicine to control my stomachache and diarrhea. Anxiety made me lose my appetite and weight.

It was not just my course work that upset me. My job as a secretarial helper at an English Language Institute made me feel like I couldn't do anything. I didn't know how to make a transparency in a copy machine, how to use a coffeemaker, or how to use a typewriter. I did know how to use a computer, but I didn't understand the secretary's instructions as to what I should do with the computer. The worst—I almost jumped off my chair whenever the phone rang. I felt as if I was an idiot sometimes. I felt totally out of sync with others. In Taiwan I am very good at reading people and I learn fast. At my job, well, everything seemed unclear.

I had personal problems, too. I got a letter from the office of my apartment which accused me of delaying my payment. From my point of view, the letter was extremely rude. I had an impulse to tell her that in my country, under the same situation, they will make sure if the tenants paid or not, before sending them that kind of letter. But, I repressed my feelings and said nothing. The manager just said, "I don't know what went wrong, but I will check it later." She didn't even apologize to me. She didn't remember to check either. I had to ask three times. Such experiences were difficult. Depression accumulated in my heart.

I had many such problems, but I kept reminding myself that I am using English. I am interacting with Americans. But, I was starting to dislike many of the

Americans I met. I was in trouble. Nothing was easy for me anymore.

Then one day, I sat alone in my apartment. A weird thought suddenly struck me. If I died in my apartment, nobody would know. The thought scared me. How come I put myself in a miserable situation like that? I was regretting my decision to be independent from the Taiwanese community. Nevertheless, deep down, I knew I had to take responsibility for my decision. One thing was for sure, I did not want to give up.

So, I decided to spend some time exploring myself and analyzing my weaknesses and strengths and creating strategies to reduce some of the stress and anxiety. I listed ten reasons not to study so hard, and read them aloud before I went to bed each night. When I felt anxious, I used meditation to calm down. I also talked to classmates who had similar problems and were willing to share their feelings with me. In addition, I wrote never-mailed letters to tell my best friend my deep feelings about everything. By the end of October I could sleep at night and didn't feel anxious as often. As time passed, I learned how to handle course requirements in more effective ways. I still lacked confidence to express my opinions in class, though. But, I accepted it as part of me. Then, I felt much better.

In the meantime, I tried to understand American culture. I watched TV shows such as "20/20," "60 Minutes," and some soap operas. I observed Americans I encounter in my daily life, and asked questions when I was confused about Americans' behavior. I stopped comparing everything to my experience in Taiwan, and I made a friend with Eileen, an American student in one of my classes. She was interested in Taiwanese food, so I cooked for her, and our friendship grew closer.

Gradually, I discovered some things in American culture that I really appreciated. As for things that I disagree with, I simply accepted them as cultural differences. They were not right or wrong. Just different.

But, the most fortunate thing was I got a wonderful host family at the end of October. The lady who "adopted" me was very thoughtful, optimistic, and supportive. I felt free to tell her about my feelings, my family, and some things about Taiwan. I thought she understood me from both what I said and what I didn't say, which was really beyond my expectations. We went to see movies, cooked, did gardening, went shopping, and celebrated holidays together. Her daughter and grandson lived near by, and they also became good friends of mine. The warmth and support I got from her family were invaluable.

Because of time, understanding more about American people's reactions to me, change in my attitude, increased certainty about what to expect from professors and interaction in classrooms, and the support from my host family, Eileen, and other friends, discomfort gradually diminished, and I have become very happy.

I tried hard to survive, but I did more than just survive. I now have an interesting life in America that will be a part of me for the rest of my life. ■

The Nursing Home—A Student from Taiwan Adopts a Grandpa at a Nursing Home

In the next narrative, a third-year undergraduate sociology major continuously tried to find opportunities to experience American culture. She tells us about one of these experiences, that of adopting an American grandfather at a nursing home.

The sky was blue, and I was cheerful. On my way home from school, I dropped into the YMCA to look at the bulletin board to see if there were any activities that I could participate in. I stared at a notice, *Adopt a Grandpa*. It was an interesting thought. A grandpa, adopted? I had heard of "adopt a son," but how it can be—a grandpa adopted? I then looked at the photos of the nursing home and all the old people sitting around. I thought they must be lonely and need someone to talk to.

The pictures of the nursing home came to my mind again and again. I kept thinking about what I heard in Taiwan about old people in America. I learned that they put them in nursing homes and don't take care of them at home, like we do. How sad! Why do Americans abandon their old people? Why do they send them to such an awful place? Don't they love their old people?

But, then I thought about what I learned in my cultures class, and I wondered. Maybe I don't understand like Americans? Maybe I should learn more? Why not adopt a grandpa!

I became a volunteer several days later and adopted a grandpa who sat on a wheelchair day after day. He was a very nice man. He showed me photos of his wife and friends. He told me that he had no children and his wife died. Most of his friends also passed away. Is this a cruel penalty for the last survivor?

During the months that I visited, I met other grandpas and grandmas at the nursing home. Some of them had children and grandchildren who visited them, and some didn't have anyone. They were all alone, like my grandpa. But, I could see that all needed help. They had Alzheimer's disease or other disease.

I could understand why my adopted grandpa had to be in the nursing home. He had nobody to take care of him. But, I wondered about other people. Why are they living here when they could live with their children? I think they could have happier life. But, sometimes when my grandpa was sleeping I talked with a very nice woman. She has problems walking, but she could do things by herself. She has three children who visit her. So, I asked her why she lives in the nursing home, not with one of her children. She explained that many American like to be independent, and she liked to live alone, even after her husband died. Then she broke her hip and fell down a lot, and she started to have a lot of problems to live alone. And then she said something I will always remember: "I love my children and I want them to be happy. I don't want them worry about me and have to take care of me all the time. That would make me feel bad. So, I came here to live. It is my choice. Nobody made me come here."

I think I learned something about Americans at the nursing home. Maybe I don't really understand everything. But, I can have stronger feeling about grandpas and grandmas in nursing homes. They want to be independent, and some American grandpas and grandmas don't want to live with their children. They like to live alone, and if they get too old and not in good condition, they move to place like this nursing home to live. This is so different from Taiwan, but Taiwan is changing. Some old people have to stay in a nursing home, too.

My American grandpa died a few months ago. I was so sad. I liked him very much. One day I went to visit him, and the nurse said he died. I left with an empty feeling inside me. ■

Medieval Art: Exceeding My Expectations—A Student from China Surpasses Her Academic Expectations

The next narrative shows how a student was able to meet the challenge of a difficult academic course.

One thing I feel successful about is the art history class I took, which gave me a lot of confidence to go on with my studies. One of the requirements for my degree in art is medieval art. I didn't like the class at all at the beginning, but I had no choice. The class was tough for me because it was about Europe, religions, and historical stuff. I knew nothing about them—totally new to me.

We had so much reading! Every week the professor assigned us so many pages to read! It was a lot, so students complained. I was the only foreign student in that class, and this made it even harder for me, but all the students in that class felt the course was so hard. For me, the reading was so dense that I really couldn't understand it. I spent all my time reading. I read till very late at night every day and also tried to write my required reflective papers on the readings.

I also had to submit a big paper and give a presentation based on the paper in front of the class. This counted as 60 percent of the final grade. I spent a lot of time on that paper. I worried about everything. I worried that I couldn't pass the class.

I had to find my own way to handle the difficult situation. I told myself, "You can find your own way. You can make it." The professor's requirement for that final paper, I decided, was not that tough. We could write something about an art period with some ideas and analysis, but we couldn't copy somebody else's work.

I came up with an idea and tried to connect something from ancient China to the Western world. In my study, I did find something about Nestorians. This group of people was ancient Christianity of the fifth century. They went to China and spread religion along the silk route during the Tang period in fifth century. Later on, they totally disappeared and only left some relics and artifacts. Now historians can trace them from manuscripts, gravestones, and some bronze crosses.

I was interested in this group of people who spread Western religion in ancient China, so I wrote an abstract and showed it to the professor. She was excited and encouraged me. This gave me—how do I say—a positive attitude! I started my research, but it was hard, for it is not a big area and not many people really study it. However, I did an online search and discovered that a bunch of people wrote papers for conferences about this group of people.

In order to get in touch with them, I tried to find their contact information and found email address for some. Finally, I sent many email with my abstract to these people to get information for my research project. I got a lot of responses from these people. They were really nice. Among these people, I emailed a professor who organizes an international conference about Nestorian study. That conference is held every three years. Based on my abstract, he invited me to present my paper at this conference. Wow! I was so surprised!

I completed my research and wrote the paper for the course. I also presented the paper in front of the class, and everyone liked it very much. I was so happy to earn an A on my research and in the course. In fact, I was surprised about my grade because many of my American classmates, who speak and write better English, didn't get an A. Even later on, they complained about the tough class.

When the course ended, my classmates relaxed and had fun. But, I didn't stop working on the paper because of the conference. I revised it and made it more professional. I was very motivated to do this because the conference organization paid my airfare, accommodation, and everything!

I benefited a lot from writing the paper because I learned how to search for relevant information, how to organize a paper, how to make an argument, and how to prove my point of view. But, most of all, I benefited because I felt successful. I gained a lot of confidence in myself and in studying at this American university. ■

As the narratives in Chapters 2 to 6 illustrate, most international students progress through a series of phases as they adapt to life in the United States. The chart on page 74 summarizes these general stages.

Stages of Cultural Adaptation: Emotional Reactions to the Unfamiliar

PREPARATION: International students are excited and/or sad in their preparation to move to the United States to study and live.

INITIAL EXPERIENCES: International students discover the loss of familiar surroundings and ways of doing things. They have a variety of new experiences, and most are highly excited about being in the United States. Some feel euphoric and are delighted to have new experiences. Others feel threatened and question their decision to study in the United States.

ONGOING INTERACTION AND CHALLENGES: As international students experience more and more of the new culture, challenges emerge. Students are challenged by physical environmental changes, language limitations, and different academic demands, as well as understanding the multitude of cultural cues that signal how to behave during everyday interaction. They are also challenged by having to use new behavior in their daily interaction, and may be bothered by having to face ways of doing things that conflict with their own personal values. Emotions may vacillate between extremes of excitement and depression. Some students start having stronger emotional reactions to ongoing experiences.

CULTURE SHOCK: Ongoing interaction and challenges can emotionally and physically tax the student, resulting in culture shock. Students show emotional symptoms such as depression, anxiety, homesickness, helplessness, and confusion. Some students eat or drink compulsively, sleep a lot, exaggerate cleanliness, feel irritable, withdraw, stereotype, and become hostile toward people in the host culture.

ADJUSTMENT: Most students realize they need to adjust to the American way of doing things. However, some have too many conflicts with values and ways of behaving and cannot fully adjust. Some do adjust enough to participate in the culture, but they become comfortable and do not want to go much beyond the minimum (attend classes, eat in the cafeteria, shop). They do not venture into the larger world outside of their immediate context. Other international students move into the larger community where they make friends with Americans, change their ways of interacting, and adapt to American values and ways of doing. Some even become bicultural.

PART 2
REFLECTIVE QUESTIONS 〰️〰️

1. Have you ever left home to live somewhere else? If so, what were your expectations? Did the place meet your expectations? What was it like for you to leave emotionally? Did you have a sad farewell, a happy one, or a little of both?

2. In Chapter 3, a student from Taiwan expressed her problem with listening comprehension and with her ability to express herself in English when she first arrived. Do you think that this is a problem for other international students? If so, why?

3. What is a cultural cue? What are examples of cultural cues that you can identify in the narratives in Chapter 4? Can you think of any other cultural cues from your daily life? How do some of these cultural cues differ across cultures?

4. Chapter 4 includes a narrative about a Japanese student's innocent lie. What do you think about this lie? What do you think about the American's reaction to the lie? Is it ever appropriate to lie in American culture? If you know other cultures, or are from another culture, is it ever appropriate to lie?

5. What is the difference in cultural protocol between the American's and Lily's way of taking messages on the phone (Chapter 4)? What about in your experience? Have you ever learned a different cultural protocol for using the phone? What was it?

6. The story of Roger and the personality changes he experienced while going through culture shock (Chapter 5) was written by his American girlfriend. At the time that Roger was experiencing culture shock, his girlfriend couldn't understand why his mood and behavior had changed so dramatically. Why do you think she couldn't understand this change?

7. Have you or people you know ever experienced culture shock? What was this experience like?

8. Chapter 6 includes a narrative by the Taiwanese student who adopted a grandfather at a nursing home as a way to learn more about American culture. Can you think of other ways that international students can learn about Americans by becoming participant observers, as the student from Taiwan did?

9. Chapter 6 includes a narrative by a Taiwanese student who decided to live away from the Taiwanese community at her university. What do you think about this? What were her reasons for doing this? Are they legitimate reasons?

PART 3

Beyond Phases: The Complexity of Cultural Adaptation

The theme of Part 3 is the complexity of cultural adaptation. Chapter 7 illustrates one facet of this complexity: the dynamic and changing nature of cultural adaptation. Each international student adapts to his or her new culture and surroundings in an individual way; students do not necessarily follow a linear progression in how they adjust. Cultural adaptation is also complex in that it can raise awareness of values conflict, as well as identity issues, topics that are addressed in Chapter 8.

CHAPTER 7

Regression and Immediate Shock

The stages of cultural adaptation should not be viewed as a linear progression. Students do not pass through the stages in the same order, and students do not necessarily pass through each stage. Rather, as the narrative by a student from Indonesia illustrates, some students initially feel well adapted, only to find themselves regressing to old feelings of culture shock. Others, such as the student from Saudi Arabia, feel culture shock soon after arriving.

Meatball Sub—A Student from Indonesia Finds Herself Experiencing Renewed Culture Shock

A talented sophomore from Indonesia wrote the first narrative. When she wrote this touching story, she had been in the United States for more than a year, had experienced and recovered from culture shock in her process of adapting to the new culture, had many friends and happy times, and thought she had adapted. However, a new experience working at an on-campus deli triggered previous feelings of confusion, help-lessness, self-doubt, and inadequacy.

"I can't wait. How interesting! How exciting!" That was what I was thinking when I was hired to work in the Hub Rock Deli. I was filled with great energy and motivation to start my first job in the U.S., although I didn't have the slightest idea about what I was supposed to do!

The day arrived. There were three other students, two girls and one boy. They were talking and laughing which made me feel a little lonely, and I wished that they would come to talk with me. But my wish was just a wish; that never happened. Then the manager came into the room. He asked a student who worked there to teach me what to do.

I read her name tag: "Erin." I looked at her and smiled. I tried to be friendly. Unfortunately, she didn't seem to care at all. "Don't worry," I said to myself, "maybe she just didn't see that you were smiling at her."

"Okay, come with me," the assigned student suddenly said. Then, for a short time, she explained my job, including the names of every food item to make a sub and directions on how to make one.

"She speaks too fast!" I moaned to myself. "How can I understand the way to make a meatball sub if I can't understand what she is saying!" Before I knew it, she had finished explaining how to make the sandwich and I realized that I hadn't been paying attention. Rather, I had been thinking about my poor English! "Oh no!" I said to myself. "What am I going to do?! I have to be able to make this sandwich within a few minutes from now!"

I thought about asking her to explain the procedure again, but I said nothing. I didn't want to make her feel bad towards me. So I just stood there in silence, my heart beating quickly.

After she walked away, I reviewed what I thought she said. I walked to the table and picked up a long roll. I opened the cooler door and tried to remember what she told me: "This is a meatball sub. You have to put the cheese inside the roll where it is split in the middle, then the meatballs on the cheese."

"Okay," I whispered to myself, "I can do that." But, I wondered about how many slices of cheese. So, I walked over to her and asked, "How many slices of cheese do I put on the bread?"

The girl looked at me with a bothered expression and said, "Whatever. Just cover the inside of the roll. Here, I'll show you." She grabbed four slices of cheese, placed them inside the long roll, and then said, "Just put six meatballs on the cheese." She then put the roll and cheese back in their respective places.

It was 12:30 PM, and it was time to begin. I was ready for the job (or should I say, I *had* to be ready for the job!).

"Can I help you?" I said to the first customer in a voice that I am sure sounded much too loud and a pitch higher than I usually speak.

I expected to be able to understand what the customer would say, but I couldn't! He repeated the order three times, when I finally realized that all he wanted was some chicken nuggets. "Oh my," I thought, "why is my listening so bad!" I had to ask each new customer questions in order to understand the order, and this took a lot of time. It was obvious that the lines in front of the other workers were moving much faster than mine. Customers even moved out of my line and into another one.

I gave one customer two cheeseburgers when she ordered a double cheeseburger. I couldn't tell the difference between a chicken sandwich and a chicken sizzler. I forgot to put the pretzel into the microwave before I gave it to the consumer until he complained about the cold pretzel.

I was doing a horrible job! Panic, exhaustion, and other bad feelings came to me little by little. I was getting disappointed with the job and with my English. Where is the energy that I had before I started?

Then, a girl came to me and ordered, "Meatball sub, please."

I instantly perked up. "Ah, I can do this one. This is my specialty!"

But, then she added, "Just with cheese and a lot of sauce."

As I walked over to get a roll, I felt confused. "What? What did she say? What did she mean? What is sauce?" I had never heard this word before! So, I walked back to the counter and asked her, "I'm sorry, what did you say?"

"I want a meatball sub, just with cheese and sauce."

I still didn't understand! I was startled. "You want a meatball sub, right?" I asked as calmly as I could, trying to hide the panic.

"Yes!"

"Just a meatball sub!" I told myself, "Forget about the details. Just make a meatball sub, give it to her, and be finished!"

So, I took that long roll and opened the cooler. I started remembering what Erin had done before. "Okay. Four slices of cheese." I placed them inside the roll. "Now, six meatballs." I picked up a label and carefully dipped into the red liquid and, one by one, scooped out six meatballs, making sure to knock the red liquid off each meatball before putting it into the roll. I put exactly six of them on the cheese. After that, I took a box, and packed the meatball sub quickly. Then, almost running, I came back to the girl and gave it to her.

"Thanks," she said as she took the sub and walked away.

"See!" I said to myself. "That wasn't so hard!"

But, a few minutes later, as I was busy with another customer, the girl came back with the meatball sub in her hand.

"Can I get more sauce?" she said with a clouded face.

I took the meatball sub with confusion. "What should I do with this sub?" I still didn't know what *sauce* was!

As I didn't know what to do, I looked around the serving area, and I focused on one of the old women who had worked there a long time. "Excuse me," I said to her. "Could you help me? I don't understand what I have to do with this meatball sub."

She looked at me for a second, then took the sub. She walked to that girl. "What do you want with this thing?" she asked the girl.

"Please put more sauce on it."

I saw the old woman's face cloud over with confusion. "What do you mean by *more sauce*? You mean this meatball sub doesn't have sauce?"

The girl in line was getting angry. "It is very easy! I just want a meatball sub with cheese and sauce! No meatball! That's all!"

A very bad feeling came over me. Even though she was not angry with me, I was the cause of that problem. But, then I saw that the old woman understood the girl. I followed her to the container on the stove where I got the meatballs. She picked up a label and scooped some thick red liquid. "This is what the girl wants," she said.

"Okay! Okay! So, that is the *sauce*! Now I understand!" I thought.

Then the old woman opened the box with the girl's sub in it. It seemed that the girl had thrown all the meatballs away. There was only the cheese left inside the roll.

"Oh my!" the old woman suddenly shouted. She turned her head and looked directly at me. "How many slices of cheese did you put in here?"

"Four, why?" I answered innocently.

"No, no! You can't do that! Just put two slices of cheese in the roll!"

"Oh really?" I was shocked. "I'm sorry. I didn't know about that."

"It's too many slices. Don't let the manager see you do this. He will fire you!"

"I'm sorry. I didn't know. Okay. I will only put two slices of cheese in each sub." I didn't want to put the blame on Erin who had taught me to put the cheese in the sub roll. "I really didn't know." I kept trying to convince the woman.

She ladled out some sauce and then gave the sub to the girl. Then, the old woman walked into the kitchen. I heard her say to her co-workers in a fairly loud voice, "That new girl put four slices of cheese on the meatball sub. Can you believe that! Maybe I will tell the manager and get her fired!" Everyone laughed.

But, I felt very bad. I felt that it was one of the worst times in my life. I was very sad.

Then, someone tapped me on my shoulder. I turned my head.

"Are you okay?" another worker asked me in a friendly, caring way.

"Yeah, I'm okay." I forced a smile.

"Don't worry about it," the worker said. "That woman is always ranting about something. It's usual. Just stay away from her, and you will be alright."

I nodded my head, smiled, and pretended to clean a table.

Slowly, a teardrop rolled down one of my cheeks. ■

From Day One—A Student from Saudi Arabia Is Jolted by U.S. Culture as Soon as He Arrives

For most international students it takes time and new experiences within the culture before culture shock surfaces. However, the next narrative shows that some students experience culture shock within a very short time after arriving in the new culture.

Before I came to America, I really didn't think it would be difficult to adjust to a new culture. "I will keep an open mind," I thought. But, right from the start I had one surprise after another, and I began to feel culture shock from the very first day. In fact, I was so shocked, I almost returned to Saudi Arabia on the second day of my stay in the U.S.

My sudden shock began at the airport in Washington, DC. Before I came to America, I imagined that everything would be very modern and new. Believing this, I was surprised to see an old small two-propeller engine plane. I was even more surprised when they told me to get into it! This plane would take me to West Virginia. The pilot and assistant carried my bags into the plane, and they helped the passengers to board and started the engine. It was so loud I had to cover my ears. The plane bounced around in the sky when gusts of wind hit us, and my stomach almost flew out my mouth when we suddenly plunged, then became level again. I thought that this plane would certainly fall from the sky somewhere in a forest and that my fate was to die in America that day. By the time we landed, I was physically and emotionally exhausted.

After we landed, I got my luggage from a small building and walked outside. I stood looking around, and even though I notified the college about my arrival, there was no one waiting to meet me. I also realized I had no idea how to get to the college. After standing for ten minutes hoping someone would suddenly call out my name, I decided to call the college. I saw a phone. But, when I picked up the receiver, I got no dial tone. So, I simply stood there looking at the phone. I had no idea how to use it, and I felt discouraged. I wondered why simple things suddenly became so difficult.

Luckily, a man asked me if I needed help, and I held out a piece of paper with a phone number and pointed to the phone. He understood my problem, and he deposited coins and dialed the number; he then gave me the phone and left. A woman from the language institute answered the phone.

The conversation was difficult. I really could not understand what the woman said to me most of the time, but I was able to understand, "Take a taxi." My next challenge was to find a taxi, so I went into the airport terminal where I saw a woman at a counter, and I said, "Taxi?" She pointed to a yellow phone. But, there were no buttons on the phone, so I thought she was making fun of me. I was frustrated and asked her how to use a phone without buttons. She told me that if I lift the receiver, someone on the other end will answer the phone. It was easy, and I felt embarrassed. I talked to someone on the other end, and I didn't understand a word of what he told me. But, I was able to communicate that I was at the airport and needed a taxi.

When the taxi arrived, the driver already had four passengers with him. But, he told me to get in the back seat. There were already three women in this small back seat, and I didn't want to get in. But, I knew I could not communicate with this taxi driver, so I got into the back seat where I sat tightly pressed against a young woman. I was upset about this and embarrassed. This was not proper. I was also upset that I did not have the taxi to myself. In my country, when a person calls for a taxi, that person will be the only passenger in the taxi. If the driver wants to take more passengers, he should ask permission from the first passenger.

The taxi cab was almost falling apart. The road was worse than the taxi. It was narrow and uneven, and it had potholes, an expression I learned that day because the drivers cursed them. I was convinced that I was in the wrong place. In my country, the best road is the road that goes to and from the airport.

Finally, the taxi driver dropped me off at the door of the language institute. I was exhausted and hungry as I had not eaten since early that morning, and all I wanted was some food and sleep. But, my first day ordeal was not yet over.

I soon found myself talking with three teachers. They were all young and female, and two of them looked younger than me. I was surprised and expected the worst to come. I was not used to talking or being with young women, and I responded to some of their questions formally and without looking at their faces, as this is impolite in my culture. I felt tense and exhausted. I wondered why I had come to this place. I was sure I had made a big mistake.

Finally, I was happy to know that I could go to my dorm, and I would have a room to myself. The assistant director asked one of the young teachers to take me to the dorm. The teacher was beautiful and nice, and she tried to chat with me, but I was really embarrassed to talk with a young lady privately. I also was not familiar in seeing women drive, but now I was with a woman in her own car. I kept silent looking out of the window. I tried to smile, but I felt as if I only had a foolish grin on my face. I don't believe I understood anything she said.

We arrived at the dorm, and the young lady talked with the receptionist, and she arranged everything for me. Finally, after saying goodbye to the young lady, I had a room and I could rest. But, I was more hungry than tired so I left the room to look for a place to eat. I remember that I was afraid to order food in a restaurant because of my poor English and because I thought they might give me food that contained pig products. As a devout Muslim, I wanted to avoid pork. So, I was happy to discover a supermarket where I bought bread and some tomatoes. That was my meal for the day. But, it was enough for me. I knew I had to live on a severe diet. After I ate, I slept for about an hour.

Feeling somewhat rested, I decided to go to the TV room. All the chairs were occupied, and one girl was watching TV while lying on her belly and playing with her feet. I was astonished by seeing this girl. I thought that she must be the worst girl in the dorm. Even the worst girls don't do that in my country. I decided that it was better for me to withdraw to my room than to see this obscene scene. So, I left the TV room, and as I walked back to my room, I saw a half naked girl come running out of her room. There was loud music and the girl was laughing and shouting at her friends. I was suddenly shocked again! I knew that I had come to the wrong place. All I wanted to do is leave, to go back to Saudi Arabia, and I decided that in the morning I would tell the assistant director of the language institute that I was going home.

Luckily for me, the assistant director convinced me to stay for two weeks "to test the waters," as she said it, before making my decision to leave. Things did get better for me. I never got used to the young students in the dorm, but I learned a lot of English, went on to earn an M.A. degree, am presently in a doctoral program, and have met and studied with some talented teachers who genuinely cared about me, my culture, and my learning. ■

CHAPTER 8

Values Conflict and Issues

The four narratives in Chapter 8 address issues related to value conflicts. A student from Kenya finds abundant opportunities to work and succeed financially in the United States but encounters racism among some Americans. A student from Niger copes with unceasing problems with a person in the next apartment and with the staff in the apartment business office. A student from Grenada struggles with what it means to be fat in Grenada and the United States, and a Saudi Arabian student faces values conflicts over punctuality and supporting a troubled friend.

 ### Half-Adjusted — A Student from Kenya Questions Her Identity as Her Emotions Straddle Two Countries

The first narrative demonstrates denial. The student apparently believed she had fully adapted to the new culture, but her words and mood shifts throughout her narrative clearly show that she had not. Her breakdown in fully adapting raises other issues. One concerns her identity as a Kenyan and the racial tension she felt in American culture. She also had an issue with trusting some Americans, as well as whether or not she would stay in America after she completed her education.

When I came to America from Kenya, I didn't know anybody. It was hard to socialize. I didn't know how to get with it. And, it was so cold! I was gaining weight. My face was breaking out. I had a lot of pimples. I came here, and the pimples were coming from every direction—whup, whup, whup, whup! I was so ugly. I felt hopeless. I went through mood swings. I came home and slept. I didn't know what I wanted. I was so depressed.

But, I started adjusting. It was getting warmer. I got a "not entirely ticked off attitude." But, then, I really changed. I was always afraid of being myself. Now I can be myself, but I don't go around trusting people. I think I was naïve.

I've learned from being in America that when somebody is rude to you, you have to pretend you've not noticed it, and you overlook it and go on. The other day at work, I told a guy something and I thought I was helping him out, and he was like, "I know what I'm doing." And, I was like, "Oh, is that so?" So, I found myself being rude back, and that's what I don't want to be. To be honest, I don't want to be Americanized.

To me, being "Americanized" is being rude. It's being arrogant. It's being self-centered. It's being selfish. It's being overbearing, controlling, ignorant. To be honest, it's being ignorant. Yes, America has its good side. It has clean water, clean roads, a lot of money, and maybe I've been with the wrong people, but so far they haven't, like, shown me something I really like.

You know, I'm more open and more confident. I want to be more confident of myself as a woman, as a Christian, as a girl. And, maybe, yeah, America has helped me to have more confidence, so it's not all bad. And, staying here would be because it has better opportunities in terms of education, job opportunities. What else? The American economic system, healthcare, and all that stuff!

But, I don't want my child to grow up here; my child will have a hard time here. She would be a half-caste. But, at home (in Kenya), you know, they don't care. People there will think she is so sweet, you know. My kid won't have a problem being black. She won't. I never realized I was black until I came to America, to be honest.

I always knew I was a woman, that's all. Being a black wasn't really a problem, but when I came here, I realized I am a black woman. I'm black and I'm African. I'm black and African. Like, white people are afraid of me. It's like, one minute they'll see me moving a gun and shooting them or something. I have to give in to stereotypes. It's just when they hear me, like when I open my mouth and say something, their attitude is different. I don't want my kid to grow up in such a place where they're always [having this kind of problem]. She's black so she's entitled to live in a ghetto. She's black so she's not allowed to shout or talk loudly. I know that black people do that but other people also. I see white girls and white guys talking on the road, shouting, using, you know, profane language, but because they are white, it's okay. But, if you see, like, black guys, black girls shouting and talking loudly, it's wrong. But, at home in Kenya we do it, and nobody will [say or think anything]. ■

A Noisy Neighbor and Racial Slurs—A Student from Niger Feels Constant Animosity in His Apartment Building

The next narrative shows that racial issues are quite real for some students. In this narrative a student from Niger found himself living in an apartment with a very noisy neighbor who turned out to be racist. The

West African student also discovered that the apartment office manager and staff were not very helpful in resolving his plight.

I am living in a dorm, and I live next door to a noisy person. He comes back at midnight and plays loud music—full blast. At first I did not complain because during international student orientation we were advised not to confront the person directly but to call the police or talk to the management.

So, I complained to the apartment manager. But, the noise continued. So, I complained again. The noise got worse. This guy came back to his apartment drunk every night, sometimes with friends, and they played loud music and had a party. The problem is the walls are paper thin, and I can hear everything. I can't study, and I can't sleep. But, management did nothing to stop him from making noise.

One day, the assistant manager happened to be passing by when the music was on full blast. He knocked on my door and asked me to ask my neighbor to lower the music. I wondered why the assistant manager didn't ask him, but I went ahead and knocked on the noisy neighbor's door. The assistant manager stood behind me, writing down notes as I talked to the neighbor. The guy turned down his music and I actually got a good night's sleep for the first time in a long time.

But, the next (Sunday) morning, the guy started calling my name and insulting me. On Monday night he started banging on the wall between us—*Bang, bang, bang!* He yelled profane language and kept saying, "Hey n***** from Africa. Wake up! Wake the f*** up! Wake up, black guy from Africa!" He repeated the same thing again and again, and I said to myself, "What's wrong with this guy?" I banged on his wall once or twice and yelled, "Shut up! Leave me alone!" But, he just banged more loudly.

After he started calling me names, I saw that it was becoming serious. So, I went to report the incident to the apartment manager and her assistant. They looked at me kind of in a strange way, but I think they understood.

Well, the next day I found an eviction notice in my mailbox. I went to the office and demanded to know why I was being evicted. It did not make sense to me. I was the one who complained about my neighbor and I ended up being evicted. Apparently the noisy guy in the next apartment told the manager lies about me, that I was banging on his wall and yelling at him.

Why did they believe him and not me? The misunderstandings and issues may be because I am black and African. It certainly seems so. But, I stayed in the room. They could not evict me because I paid my rent on time, and I tape recorded the neighbor yelling at me and playing loud music. So, they finally believed me. But, nobody in the manager's office has apologized and people in there still ignore me. Even when I greet people, with no negative motives, they turn their faces as if I want something from them. It is a very hostile place to live. ■

"She Looking Good!"—A Student from Grenada Struggles with What It Means to Be Overweight

The next narrative shows how a student faced a values conflict over the perception of what it means to be overweight.

Although this value is slowly changing in Grenada, when I grew up there, stout people were, and still are for the most part, admired because it's a sign of happiness and well being. People say that trouble makes people skinny and happiness makes them fat. In Grenada they say, "she looking good!" which really means she's added some weight, she's gotten a little fatter, she's nice and fat, and so forth. I grew up with a stout grandmother, and for years I literally prayed that I'd put on some weight so I could look as good as her. Some people used to tell me not to worry, that I'd "pick up"—that is, pick up some weight when I get older, and I waited for that day to come. I used to be teased in school for having no "bam-bam" [no butt]. I became a little excited about coming to America simply because I thought I'd be able to eat a lot of food and gain weight.

Anyway, boy was I shocked to find out that Americans diet weekly and shun fat people. But before I found that out, I would get into the habit of staring at fat people in school. I remember watching a classmate of mine everyday, simply because she was fat, and I wanted to just acquire half of her size. I used to wonder how happy she must have been, thinking that she was probably strong, well rested, eating nice food, eating a lot of food. I also thought that she probably had nice stout parents and brothers and sisters.

One day I went to history class and proceeded to continue admiring this fat classmate. That day, during class in front of everyone, the girl yelled out, "What the hell are you staring at?" That scared the crap out of me! I realized not only that I shouldn't stare at people, but also that it's not cute to be fat.

Since that experience I stopped staring at people who are fat, but I have not totally given up my admiration for them. I know that it is healthier to be slim, but a part of me still admires them. I also wonder why so many Americans shun stout people. Do they think they are better than them because they are not fat?

I guess that I can now understand what it means to be fat in two cultures, and this has taught me that each person, skinny or fat, needs to be judged by what is in their heart and their mind, not on what they look like. ■

A Different Concept of Time— A Student from Saudi Arabia Is Challenged by a Different Culturally Based Concept of Time

The fourth narrative shows a student in a quandary over values related to the use of time. His cultural background includes, as Hall (1959, 1998) has shown, a *polychronic* use of time, valuing flexibility with time. This meant making a friend's problem a higher priority than punctuality for a meeting.

I find it interesting that a lot of people I meet in the United States pay so much attention to time. For example, I have heard Americans use many expressions related to time. They save time, spend time, waste time, kill time, lose time, run out of time, find time, and have a good time. At first I thought that this attention to time was simply interesting. But, I soon realized that it is more than just interesting. I had to pay attention to time if I wanted to adjust myself to American life.

One of the things I have realized is how important it is to be on time for meetings. I learned this the hard way. I met a friend on the way to a scheduled meeting with one of my professors. My friend was having a problem and wanted my advice. By the time we finished our talk, I was fifteen minutes late for the meeting, and when I came to my professor's office, I found him talking with another student. I waited outside his office, but after the other student left, he looked at me with a stern expression and said something like, "It is important to be on time for your appointments with me. I am very busy." When I apologized and explained about meeting my friend, I was surprised by the professor's reaction. He asked me, "Which is more important? Being on time for your appointment or chatting with a friend?" He then told me to schedule a new appointment. The way he asked indicated that he thought being on time for our meeting took priority.

After this experience, I realized that we value our use of time in different ways. In Saudi Arabia, I think it is okay to be late for a meeting if you are talking to a friend about his problem. It would be impolite to stop in the middle of such a conversation to run to a meeting. So, I am not sure what to do here. I don't want to look at my watch and say, "Oh, I'll be late for a meeting. I had better go!" But, if I don't do this, I might create a problem for myself and others. ∎

PART 3
REFLECTIVE QUESTIONS ⩗⩘⩘

1. DeCapua and Wintergerst state, "For many people experiencing culture shock, the recovery stage is slow, involving periodic crises, setbacks, and readjustments" (2004, p. 111). What do you think they mean by this statement?

2. My research assistants and I discovered that some international students, such as the student from Indonesia in Chapter 7 who was working at an on-campus deli, seemed to fully adapt, only to regress back to feelings of strong culture shock. The surprising thing is that some of those who regressed had been living in the United States for over a year. Why do you think this happens?

3. The Nigerian student in Chapter 8 unfortunately found himself living in an apartment with an extremely noisy neighbor who turned out to be a racist. He also had problems communicating the reality of his situation with the apartment manager and staff. If you had the chance, what would you advise him to do?

4. Chapter 8 illustrates an issue of being plump or stout from the perspective of a student from Grenada. What is the issue? What view do people in different cultures have about plump or heavy people?

5. What thoughts do you have about the difference between the Saudi Arabian student in Chapter 8 choosing friendship over being on time and the American professor's choosing being on time over listening to a friend's problem? Why could the Saudi Arabian's value choice become an issue for some Americans?

6. Related to Question 5, how might a student raised with one value have problems understanding or communicating with people who were raised with other values?

PART 4

Behavior That Can Encumber Successful Adaptation

The theme of Part 4 is on behavior that can hinder successful cultural adaptation. The narratives illustrate specific behaviors used by the students that did not help them adapt in a positive way. Behaviors include excessively complaining and avoiding interactions with Americans (Chapter 9), and expecting Americans to adapt to the international student's ethnocentric way of interacting and withdrawing into the expatriate community (Chapter 10).

CHAPTER 9

Complaining and Avoiding

Although most international students adapt to their new environment, some students never really do. As Storti (2001) points out, some continue to have the *ethnocentric impulse* that others are like them, and they continue to expect other people to behave as they do. This creates cultural incidents while interacting with Americans that lead them to react with anger, worry, or other negative feelings. Rather than reflecting on the incident that created the bad feelings and analyzing the behavior that possibly contributed to the intercultural communication incident, as many of the students who successfully adapt do, students who have trouble adapting often continue to complain, avoid interactions with Americans, expect Americans to adapt to their cultural ways of behaving, or withdraw into the expatriate community.

This chapter features a narrative by a German student who continuously complains even after being at a university in the United States for more than a year. It also includes a narrative by a Korean student who avoids interacting with her roommate, as well as a narrative based on a professor's observation of a student from Benin who has isolated himself and avoids interacting with Americans and other international students.

Americans Are Boring — A Student from Germany Complains That Conversations with Americans Lack Substance

The first narrative is recreated from detailed field notes and is based on a conversation I had with a student from Germany. I knew this student fairly well, and the narrative illustrates how he complained on an ongoing basis as a strategy to cope with cultural adaptation problems, a strategy that seems to do little more than irritate those around the person.

I'm an exchange student. I've been in this country for almost one year, and I am ready to go back to Germany. I like my classes and some of the professors, but I think American students are boring. I have two interesting seminars in Sociology, and sometimes we have stimulating discussions. But, when I try to talk to Americans outside class, the conversations are boring.

Here is what I mean. Last week I went to a fraternity party. There was a keg of beer, and everyone drank all day and night. But, it was not interesting for me. When I drink, I like to debate—World affairs, the Iraqi war, or other politics. Why did America attack Iraq? Why didn't America attack Afghanistan? Is oil the center of the attack? But, when I start to discuss such topics with an American, the conversation always ends quickly or the American changes the topic—"Look at that hot chick over there." "You want to order pizza?" "Did you see the (Pittsburgh) Steeler's game?" The same thing happened last week. Only one person wanted to debate topics, and he left the party early.

I mean the drinking contests are fun, and joking around is fun, but that is not enough for me. I like to debate important topics, like we do in my seminars. But, I guess Americans only like to debate in class. Boring, you know. Americans are sometimes boring. ∎

Kimchi—A Student from South Korea Avoids Her American Roommate after a Confrontation about Food

The next narrative shows how a Korean student and her American roommate had difficulty communicating. The young American had little awareness of Korean culture, and when the Korean student innocently broke the rules of kitchen etiquette by keeping containers of *kimchi* (fermented cabbage) in the refrigerator, her apartment-mate became quite upset. To some Americans, kimchi has a very strong penetrating smell. The American possibly assumed the Korean student was purposefully imposing her "putrid food" (to use the upset American's words) on her. Such miscommunication created a problem. However, the Korean student preferred to avoid addressing the problem out of fear of upsetting her apartment-mate and herself even further. Such avoidance could have made the problem escalate.

I got a new roommate, Sasha. I was excited because she was African American, and I could learn African-American English with her. It has slang and expressions I felt, well, difficult to understand. So I wanted to learn with her, and I wanted her to learn about Korea culture, too.

The first day I shared my food with her. She was very quiet for two or three days after that. And, I could not start to talk with her because she was too quiet and never talk except to ask where McDonalds and supermarket are, and she was always listening music with earphone.

I was frustrated and thought, "What was wrong with her?" And one or two weeks later, I felt she did not like me because she shutted doors with a big bang whenever she went out, and she always closed doors between the bedroom and living room whenever I came in.

I felt upset because she did not want to talk to me, and I wanted to ask her what is the matter. But, I felt my English was not enough to talk with her because her speaking was so fast and peculiar.

The biggest thing that made me upset was she put three pieces of paper with some sentences on the wall. I was trying to understand those meanings, but it was very hard to understand. So, I asked American people to tell what the meanings were. He said to me that my roommate had very negative emotion to me so it was better to move out this apartment. I only could think, "Oh! What happen to me? Why she did not like me? What should I do?"

I was so upset and so frustrated, and I could not find any reason that she did not like me. I thought I was so careful. I watched TV and listened music with a little sound, and I usually was quiet and got up early and come back apartment late. My efforts for her did not work. She gave me impression that she hated me. I could not concentrate on my studying, and sometimes I cried alone in my room.

I wanted to talk to her, but I could not say anything. Whenever I thought of her, it reminded me of her scary eye contact and her cool acts to me. Then, one day she said to me, "Come with me."

I followed her to the Residence Hall office. She started to talk very fast, and I couldn't understand what she said, but her voice was so angry. She was talking with the residence assistant, not me because she used the word *she* instead of *you*. I was so scared because I never experienced that kind of conversation.

The residence hall assistant asked me, "What's the problem?" I couldn't say anything at first. I just wanted to hide. Then, I said, "I don't know."

My roommate had angry look on her face, and started to yell. I can remember her words. "Stop this game! Your food smell very bad. Everything smell bad. It has putrid smell! I can't eat my food because it stinks from your food!" Then she looked at the assistant resident and said, "You talk to her. She makes me too angry!" Then she walked away.

"Oh! She is angry because of smell of my food!" I said to the assistant resident. I felt sorry! After I remove *kimchi* and cleaned the refrigerator, I wanted to apologize to Sasha. I wanted to explain, tell her how stupid I am. I heard that Americans don't like smell of *kimchi*. But, I didn't think about that. I only thought of my favorite traditional food. I wanted to tell Sasha this, and I wanted to tell her I will not keep kimchi in refrigerator any more.

But, I couldn't say anything to her. I kept quiet. I wanted to avoid talking to her because she didn't like me. I thought that she will notice refrigerator is clean and no more smell of *kimchi*. Surely she will notice. Maybe she did, maybe not. We never spoke again. ■

A Secret Miserable Life—
The Problems of a Student
from Benin Drive Him into

Becoming Reclusive

The next narrative is based on my observations and conversations with a student from Benin. He came to the United States on a government scholarship, and he was delighted to be in the United States when he first arrived. But gradually he became more and more withdrawn, and he avoided interaction not only with Americans but also with other international students. As his only American friend, I became more and more aware of this student's very lonely, difficult life in the United States.

first met Yves at our academic program orientation. He was sitting alone; I sat beside him. He had a big grin on his face when he shook my hand. He said with a French accent that he was very happy to be in the United States to study, but he was worried about meeting the expectations of his professors. He promised me that he would study very very hard.

Yves was in one of my fall semester graduate courses, and right from the start I could see he was timid. He was hesitant to talk with other students in the class, including other international students, all from Asian countries. He rarely contributed to class discussion unless I called on him directly, but he did turn in highly processed written homework assignments.

However, over the two months, Yves seemed to become more and more withdrawn. He also had noticeably lost weight, and he no longer grinned when we talked. Worried about him, I asked him to come to my office to talk. I had hoped I could find out more about his life and why he was becoming more and more despondent. But he said everything was fine, that he was happy and enjoyed his life here.

However, something in his eyes told me that behind the façade, Yves was having a difficult time. He likely did not want to disturb me with his problems, but I could see a silent call for help in his eyes and through his behavior. So, I decided to visit him.

Yves was quite surprised to see me at his apartment door. I didn't want to embarrass or impose on him, so I suggested we go to a nearby McDonald's for coffee and chat. And Yves opened up. In fact, he talked for two hours about his "miserable life," to use his words. He told me about his high levels of anxiety when he talks to other students and his inhibitions about talking to Americans. So, he kept to himself, studied alone, and stayed in his small apartment most of the time. He either slept a lot or didn't sleep at all depending on his mood and classroom assignments.

I could easily see that Yves felt disheartened, and as he talked and tears came to his eyes, he told me that his mother had died two weeks earlier and that he could not attend her funeral. His scholarship only gave him enough money to pay his rent and meet his personal needs, and even if he could borrow the money to go to Benin, he said he felt obligated to study.

I asked him why he didn't reach out to the International Affairs office or other international students for support, and he replied that he didn't feel comfortable doing that. He wasn't a member of the International Student Association, and he didn't want to bother anyone.

We left McDonald's and said goodbye. I watched as he walked toward his apartment, his head bowed toward the ground and his shoulders slumped. I could hear him sigh. ■

CHAPTER 10

Expecting Others to Adapt and Withdrawing into the Expatriate Community

The narratives in this chapter show how some international students expect Americans to adapt to their values and behavior. The first narrative is from an exasperated Nigerian student who gets upset about how Americans interact with him. The second narrative is from a well-intentioned student from China who uses a strategy to turn down an invitation that annoys her American friend. The third is by a Thai student who becomes disheartened after using indirect behaviors to try to communicate with her young unaware American roommate.

Hey Lady! In My Culture We Don't Do That! — A Student from Nigeria Expects Americans to Adjust to Him

The first narrative illustrates how a student expects a student dining hall supervisor to change her attitudes and behavior toward him based on the rules within his culture. Frustrated by his situation, he lashes out at the supervisor.

Here we have a lot of people who treat you inhumanely, like shouting or ordering you around. For example, I had a bad experience at Freedom Dining Hall (where I worked). A lady asked me to do something without showing me how to do it. So I took a certain detergent to clean the table. Then this lady comes around shouting, "Never use this liquid again!"

I asked her, "What I'm supposed to use?" Then instead of answering my question, she ordered me around shouting, "Don't be smart with me!"

And I told her, "Hey lady. Stop yelling at me. In my culture, we don't do that. I'm older than you—so stop yelling at me." I then went to the manager and reported the incident. I told him I was ready to quit if I was not treated with respect. These people bully people because they are ignorant. Some of these people treat people very differently and inhumanely. They don't treat people well just because they have a different culture or race.

Most of these people come from small rural towns. When they come to this larger university town, they think it is a very big city. Then they start treating people badly. You see, I do my job very well. I am old enough to do my job well and I am responsible. Like that incident. I told the lady supervisor I would quit if I was not treated well. Well, one day the same lady supervisor told me, "Leave the broom and go home."

I honestly told her, "You are a woman, and I'm a man. Come take this broom from me. Can you take it from me?"

These people have no politeness. They value themselves; that is it. Even if you tell them about your culture, they do not take it seriously. They do not understand that you are from a different culture and they are not interested. They will never try to understand you and be tolerant of you. But, I will not let them treat me badly. I will be myself, and if they don't want to learn about my culture and me, that is their problem. ■

The Invitation—A Student from China Tries to Convince Her Annoyed American Friend That *Yes* Can Mean *No*

The next narrative illustrates a communication strategy that is based on assumptions from the international student's own culture. A student is invited to an American party, and she applies a strategy from her Chinese experience (enculturation) to imply she will likely not go to the party when she says, "I am so glad that you invited me; I will try my best to come." To the Chinese student this means she will not likely go to the party. But this is not clear to her American friend, who has been raised to be more direct in her communications. As Wang, Brislin, Wang, Williams, & Chao (2000) point out, such Chinese strategies can lead to critical incidents, misunderstanding, and even long-term damage to friendships between Chinese and Americans.

Joanne, my American classmate, and I have the start of a very good relationship, I think. We talk after class and laugh a lot. So, I was happy when she invited me to a party. But, I didn't know if I could go or not because I had to study for a test. So, I said yes to her invitation in a way that means "likely, no."

Like other Chinese people, I feel it is impolite to tell someone no to her face. If we are not able to go to a party, we will never say no. Instead, we will say something like, "I am so glad that you invited me; I will try my best to come." This actually means that we will likely not go to the party.

I really wanted to go. But, I also wanted to try my best to get a good grade on my test, and that is not so easy for me. It takes me a long time to read and prepare for tests. So, I didn't go to the party. I studied for my test instead.

The next day I saw Joanne in front of the library, and I waved. She didn't wave back. She looked at me, turned around, and walked into the library. I'm sad. Usually she would have a big smile on her face, wave back, and we would meet for a few minutes to chat.

I guess I need to explain to Joanne how Chinese are so indirect so she can understand me and why I say yes when I mean no. I think if she learns about my culture, she can understand me. I think this is the best way for us to be friends. ■

Dormitory Turnoff—A Student from Thailand Gives Up Her Dream of Having American Friends

The final narrative is similar to the first two in that the semi-aware student expects her American roommate to adapt to her way of behaving. However, this narrative is different in that the overwhelmed, disheartened Thai student decides to withdraw into her home community.

Through this narrative it is easy to see that the Thai student values modesty, as do many Thais, and that she does not feel comfortable with her roommate's nudity. It is also easy to see that she doesn't appreciate her roommate's friends sitting on her bed with their shoes on, and pointing their feet at her. Her uneasiness is likely not fully at a conscious level for her, that pointing feet at someone can disturb the *khwaan* or spirit essence (Heinze, 1982; Klausner, 1993; Klausner & Klausner, 1970). Thais generally believe that 32 khwaan live within each person. The most important are those in the top of the body (the head and heart) and the worst in the bottom of the body. As such, it is important not to point one's foot at another person, especially the head, as part of this spirit essence could escape.

As shown in her narrative, this student expects her roommate to understand her indirect, high-context hints related to these problems.

DeCapua and Wintergerst explain that in high-context cultures "much of the actual message is left unsaid or implied (through the use of non-verbal behavior), and it is up to the speakers to understand the implicit information being imparted. The message itself is dependent on the context within which it is being delivered" (2004, p. 71). For the young American roommate, who grew up in a low-context cultural setting, such high-context messages escape her.

The Thai student's young American roommate is oblivious to the Thai student's high-context, indirect communicative strategy, and life becomes more and more overwhelming for the Thai student. As a result, she is disheartened and gloomy about the prospects of having American friends. Her solution is to withdraw into the Thai community where she can be comforted by those who understand her cultural background. She makes a decision that Storti (2001) points out will take her further and further away from adapting to the host culture and fulfilling her dream of having an American friend.

> I dreamed of studying in the United States ever since I was a little girl. When I was young, I loved to study English. I majored in English at Thammasat University. I loved English. I even went to language school on weekends, and I join English club at university and went to many many movie. I did not speak to my parents about going to America because it is expensive. But, they knew I want to study in the United States. So, they saved money for me. And, one day my father, he said to me, "*Luk, bai lian mahawitialai yu thii America, dai mai?*" (My child, can you go to America to study at a university?). I said, "*Dai!*" (Yes!) And, that night, I lay on my bed with my eyes open. But, I was dreaming about coming to America.
>
> I want to study hard and get my M.A. degree. I also wanted to make American friends. So, I moved into this dormitory to live with an American. My roommate, she much younger than me, a sophomore, and she had a lot

of friends. But, I try to be friendly and talk with her. And, at first, she was friendly. We ate together in the cafeteria and sometimes talked in our room.

But, one difference between her and me is I want to study a lot. I go to the library until it closes. Then, I go back to my room in the dorm. I sometimes study until 2:00 AM. Well, I try to study. But, this is not so easy. This is because my roommate has too many friends, and they like to meet in our room. They come to our room anytime, sometimes late at night, even when I am studying. They play music, talk and laugh loudly, and eat pizza, potato chips, and other junk food. I want to be polite, so I don't say anything. I think if they see me studying, they will leave. But, they don't leave. The worst is one girl who sits on my bed with her shoes on. And, she points her feet at me. I don't know why, but this bothers me a lot. In Thailand, we don't do like that. In Thailand, you know, we take shoes off in our house or dorm room. I know that in America this is not the custom. But, I feel very bad. I can't sleep because I feel dirty, and I wash my blanket too often.

I try to talk to my roommate. I try to tell her in nice way that I cannot study and that in Thailand we do not put shoes on the bed. One day I talked to my friend while my roommate was in the room. I said to my friend in a loud voice, "I wish I can study more in the room." I also said, "You know, in Thailand it is really impolite to put shoes on the bed and to point feet at someone." But, she didn't listen. Nothing changed. I get so frustrated. Now, I just leave the room and go study in the lounge. Not good. Cold. I am cold there and I hear TV.

I also get so embarrassed! My roommate, she takes off all her clothes in front of me. Everything! Even her underpants! I am so embarrassed! Thai people, we don't do that. We are very shy. But, she doesn't care. She just walks around the room like that sometimes. I want to run away!

Why can't my roommate understand my situation? I have to study a lot. It is too hard for me. And, why she doesn't listen to me? Maybe she is too young. But, I think she has no background to understand me or other foreign students. She only has her American way. She thinks all people should be like her. Or, she doesn't think about other cultures and people.

Next semester I will live with my Thai friends off campus. We will speak Thai, I know, and English will not get very good. I had a dream to have American friends. But, I don't want to have American friend now. I just want to study hard, get my degree, and go back to Thailand. ■

As the narratives indicate, international students need to make efforts to adapt and to avoid behaviors that hinder success. It is important to emphasize and reiterate, however, that the responsibility for cultural adaptation should not be placed solely on the international students. The university community also needs to be sincere and proactive in welcoming all international students and should provide a positive, helpful environment. Many universities and colleges do this through an orientation at the international affairs office and a wide variety of other programs that involve and reach out to international students. It's important that international students be made aware of the assistance and resources that are available.

PART 4
REFLECTIVE QUESTIONS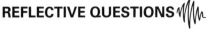

1. Have you ever known someone who continually complains? How do others around that person react to this person's complaints? How did complaining undermine the German student's adaptation?

2. Through your understanding of the narrative *Kimchi,* how did the communication problem first begin between the Korean student and Sasha? How did the problem escalate? What assumptions were made by both Sasha and the Korean student that turned out to be incorrect?

3. Have you ever been isolated from others? If so, what was it like? If not, based on the narrative about the student from Benin, what do you think it would be like to feel isolated, alone in the world?

4. The Nigerian student in Chapter 10 was upset because he was not treated with respect at the student dining hall where he works. He reacted strongly by complaining about Americans' attitudes toward people from other cultures. What did he expect Americans to do? Were his expectations reasonable?

5. What strategy did the student from China use to decline a party invitation? Why was the American upset? Would you be offended? Why or why not?

6. If you had the chance, what advice would you give to the Thai student in Chapter 10 who had communication problems with her roommate?

PART 5

Strategies and Successful Adaptation

The narratives in Part 5 focus on strategies that seem to be very beneficial in helping international students adjust to their new lives in the United States. These successful strategies include using humor and optimism (Chapter 11), observing and matching the behavior of Americans (Chapter 12), observing and reflecting on their own behavior (Chapter 13), and seeking support from the university and community (Chapter 14).

CHAPTER 11

Humor and Optimism

Research in the 1950s and 1960s (Ruben, 1987) on ways to adapt successfully to another culture emphasized personal mannerisms, such as showing respect, being courteous, gaining empathy, and being nonjudgmental. Based on his years of experience with and research on both international and American students, Kohls (1996) adds having a sense of humor and a strong sense of self, as well as being open-minded, curious, self-reliant, and perceptive. Using humor and keeping an optimistic outlook are strategies that have proven to be successful for international students in adjusting to their new surroundings.

Face Covered—A Married Couple from Syria Teaches a Child about Their Culture

The first narrative shows how a married couple from Syria used humor to teach a curious child about their culture. This narrative is based on my observation of what transpired between this relatively young couple and a young boy while waiting in the payment line at Walmart.

As I was standing in line, I saw a curious young boy, approximately seven years old and who apparently had wandered away from his parents, approach an Islamic woman and ask, "Why is your face covered?" He then looked at her husband, and asked, "Is she ugly?"

The husband laughed and said, "No. She is my beautiful wife."

The boy looked at her intently, and then asked, "Is she hiding?"

The husband smiled and answered, "No, she's not hiding, although it would be a great way to hide!"

The little boy giggled. "Is she in a Halloween costume?"

"No. This is the way she dresses. She is from Syria. Women dress like this. Her dress is called a *hijab*."

"*Hi–hi–jab*," the boy sounded out. "Where's Serial? Is it in Pennsylvania?"

"It's Syria. It's where we are from. It's a country in the Middle East."

The wife then proceeded to uncover her face and show the boy that she had absolutely no problem with her face.

The little boy smiled and his eyes twinkled.

At this point the boy's parents arrived. "There you are! We were looking everywhere for you! I hope he isn't bothering you," the mother said to the Syrian couple.

"Oh no. He is nice little boy." The husband then explained what had happened. The parents explained to the boy that there wasn't anything strange about this, but it was only a matter of different cultures and understanding.

After the boy and his parents left, I asked the Islamic couple how they felt about the encounter with the boy. They told me that they felt good about themselves and about the experiences in this American community. ■

Post 9/11—A Student from Saudi Arabia Keeps an Open, Understanding Heart toward American Suspicions

The next narrative is told by a student from Saudi Arabia after 9/11. He had arrived in the United States to study, and despite negative feelings and confusion at times, this student consistently looked at life and his experiences in the United States with optimism and good will.

I came to the U.S. as a student on December 25, 2002. I planned to stay here for at least four years as a graduate student, and as a Saudi and Muslim, I was prepared to endure special INS [Immigration and Naturalization Services] regulations after September 11th. With all this in mind, I entered the States with the intent to complete my studies and do my best to show Americans that the majority of Muslims are good people.

When I arrived at the airport lounge in JFK, I was fascinated by the Christmas lights and trees, but at the same time shocked by the sight of National Guardsmen and FBI throughout the terminal, accompanying travelers (Saudis in particular) to the INS interview areas. As I stood in front of the INS officer I remembered my mother begging me to stay in Saudi Arabia, especially at this time. For several hours I remained scared, to the point of losing my competency in English at times. Finally, I was cleared and allowed to board my flight to a small town in Ohio.

After arriving, I phoned my friend who said he would meet me. I was shocked to discover that he was waiting in the parking lot, too scared to enter, fearful of dirty looks he may receive from other people. He told me to exit the terminal and he would pass by me, and to get into the car quickly, and not to talk to anyone along the way at all.

During our drive to the university I questioned him about his behavior, to which he responded, "Are you crazy? Look at the color of your skin. You are a terrorist. You look like one."

I rejected his notion, and added that we should not buy into the stereotypes projected by the media. Although he agreed with me, he seemed frustrated. From that point on I realized that adjusting to American culture would not be an easy task, especially because of negative preconceptions propagated to the masses through the media.

I attended orientation and began exploring the university town on my own. The first few months I felt mixed emotions, ranging from fear to excitement, and even homesickness. However, the Saudi community provided me with a sense of belonging, where everyone could express their complaints, questions, jokes, and occasionally cry.

However, I wanted to go beyond the Saudi community, and I gradually made some practical steps toward immersing myself into American culture. To begin, I engaged in social activities both inside and outside my department, such as picnics, dinner parties, and field trips. I joined the Conversation Partners program, sponsored by the International Affairs office. Through this program I got to know several Americans. I also made friends with American classmates, and I visited their homes during weekends or holidays. I also invited friends to my home, giving them an opportunity to experience my culture. I also became a very active member of the Graduate Student Organization in my department, as well as joined regional, national/international professional organizations.

I attended conferences and presented papers at their meetings. I also socialized with a variety of people at these meetings.

During all these experiences, I have kept a positive outlook and an open heart. I think this is why I have been able to immerse myself into American culture, make so many friends, and go well beyond my fears and anxieties about being in the States after 9/11. ■

CHAPTER 12

Observing and Matching Behaviors

Another strategy that many international students use to successfully adapt to their new culture is to observe and match the behaviors of Americans. This strategy is also used in many professional settings. For example, such matching behaviors are used by some psychotherapists to build rapport between themselves and their patients. For them, matching a patient's posture, gestures, facial expressions, slight movements, and even breathing gives them an empathetic understanding of the other person (Bandler & Grinder, 1979; Grinder, DeLozier, & Bandler, 1996; Grinder & Bandler, 1976; Rosen, 1982). As the narratives illustrate, observing and matching are behaviors that can be very helpful.

Do As They Do—A Student from Argentina Imitates North American Ways of Walking, Eating, and More

The first narrative illustrates how a student from Argentina became aware of her nonverbal behavior, especially the interpersonal distance and touch behaviors she used when interacting with North Americans.

As Chong and Baez (2005) point out, most Latinos, including those from Argentina, keep a personal space of "about 14 or 15 inches.... This contrasts sharply with European Americans' preferred distance of between 18 inches and four feet" (p. 55). They add, "A person who is not familiar with Latino culture may consider the distance intrusive or misinterpret the behavior as a desire to establish personal intimacy" (p. 55). As this next narrative illustrates, such use of touch behavior can also be misinterpreted within parts of the United States.

Having become aware of such misinterpretations of her behavior, this student decided to observe and imitate the distance North Americans stand apart from each other, as well as their greeting and touch behavior and more.

I remember my first interaction with a group of North Americans three days after I arrived here. My parents are friends with a professor and his wife at the university where I am studying, and they invited me to eat at a restaurant with them and a few of their North American friends. I lived near the restaurant, so we decided to meet there. When we met at the entrance of the restaurant, I kissed everyone in the group. They were surprised, and I was so embarrassed because I knew there was something wrong. When I got home, I asked my new friend from Costa Rica, who lived in the U.S. a couple years, about my greeting. She said that non-Latino people are not so used to kisses when they greet each other. Some do, but most don't.

I also experienced strange reactions from American classmates when I talked to them. I am a friendly person and like to laugh and smile. When I talk to guys, they start to, what's the expression, come on to me. I can feel a kind of sexual tension. But, some classmates seem to back away from me. My friend told me that I probably stand too close to them, and maybe I touch them too much.

This can really excite the guys, she said. She laughed and told me to be careful.

I thought this was funny. But, I also thought I should learn more about American nonverbal behavior to stay out of trouble. So, I decided to watch North Americans communicate. I sat in coffee shops, on benches, in the cafeteria, and other places, and I simply watched. I saw that they don't touch so much really. At that time, when I said hello to a friend, not a close friend, I usually touched their arm and stood close. I decided to stop doing that, except with close friends.

My watching gave me an idea. One of my professors told the class that he likes to imitate the behavior of people when he goes to a new place. He walks behind them and does what they do. He sits near them and imitates their actions (without them noticing). So, I started to follow North American women across campus. I walked the same exact way, and I was very surprised. Americans walk differently. They are all kind of different, but they all keep some distance and have the same kind of arm swing.

I learned so much by imitating these women, I decided to find a person in the cafeteria and imitate the way they eat. It surprised me. There are a lot of small differences, like the way we hold a knife. I also eat more slowly than many Americans. And some students talk a lot while they chew food.

I still like to watch people. Fun, and I learn about how to change my behavior so I can be natural, you know, fit in. ■

Timing Is Everything —
An Unsure Student from Japan
Laughs When the Audience
 ## Laughs at a Comedy Show

The next narrative is also about observing nonverbal behavior, but it is specific to matching behavior at a comedy show and shows the joy that an international student felt when becoming part of an American audience.

had a chance to see Bill Cosby live. I had not known of him at all before. When I decided to go to the show, I felt complex feelings. I thought that I could have a good experience, but at the same time, I was a little afraid that I could not understand his stage at all because of my language problem. As I wanted to have a good time, I made up my mind to do one thing. I decided to laugh whenever the audience laughed even if I did not understand why. The beginning of his talk was relatively understandable even to me. In some parts I laughed because I really thought he was funny. But, as his talk continued and topic changed, the parts that I couldn't understand increased. I remembered my decision. I laughed when I heard the person next to me laugh or when I heard laughter somewhere from my back. I also applauded when others did.

In Japan, I love to see comedy. Japanese audience laughs a lot, of course. But, it was my first time to see people clap their hands during the show to applaud every part that they really felt satisfaction. I think that Japanese do not have this kind of habit while seeing comedy. I imitated this clapping behavior as they did. During the show I found myself laughing and clapping until I was crying. I was really enjoying the show! Laughter made me happy and it probably helped me guess or feel the comedian's messages.

I thought about this experience with matching my laughing and clapping behavior. Through matching, I learned I can help myself comprehend the situation more. Especially laughter is a very important factor. Feelings of happiness seem to broaden the capacity of comprehension. ■

CHAPTER 13

Doing and Reflecting

Taking time to think about, understand, and reflect on their experiences and interactions can also lead international students to success in adapting to their new cultures. Weaver (2000b) discusses various coping mechanisms and recommends that international students understand and reflect on the process of adjustment. The more they understand the cultural adaptation process, the better they can predict stressful problems. Additionally, such understanding offers them a way to make sense of confusion, disorientation, and ambiguity.

Craig Storti (2001) frames his adaptation strategies around the concept of observation and reflection. He recommends that sojourners, including international students, observe and reflect on their reactions to cultural incidents, as these incidents can be indicators that they have not been following the interaction rules. In other words, their frustration or anger or annoyance is usually triggered precisely at the moment the locals fail to do what they expect. The idea is for international students to train themselves to become aware of their emotions, as well as catch themselves in the process of expecting the locals to behave like they do.

Students who strategically are willing to take risks by exploring new relationships and new ways of interacting will certainly discover much about American culture. More important, when international students make an effort to reflect on and evaluate their experiences, as well as to generate and try out alternative ways of interacting based on their reflections, they will make progress. Some will even go on to gain strong intercultural communication competence.

Living with a Middle-Aged American Couple — A Reflective Student-Boarder from Taiwan Alters Her Social-Interactive Behavior

The first narrative shows how a student reflected on and changed her interactive behavior while living with an American couple.

was thrilled that I was finally going to have a chance to truly experience local American culture. I'd always dreamed of joyfully and freely interacting with the local Americans since I was little. One Tuesday evening in May I moved into my new home away from home. I would be living with a middle-aged working couple, and I anticipated a warm welcome and friendly smiles.

But, Mrs. Harris opened the door, showed me to my room, and immediately went into the TV room where her husband was watching TV. When I was busy moving my things into my bedroom, the dog kept barking in the TV room, which made me feel even less welcome. I could sense indifference and unfriendliness. If this had happened in Taiwan, both of them would have greeted me and asked whether I needed some help, but they didn't. I felt a little offended.

When I settled down resting at my room, the dog ran up barking at me. Hearing its barking, Mrs. Harris came upstairs and officially introduced me to the dog to stop his hostility. Then she gave me a tour of the kitchen, the laundry room, and the bathroom. She then went back into the living room leaving me in the hall.

The next day, I got up as early as they did, seeing them off to work to show my politeness. When they were back, I would cease whatever I was doing at my room to greet them in the front door. Then I went back to my room, looking forward to their inviting me to eat dinner together. However, when I went downstairs, they already had their dinner in the TV room. Feeling disappointed, I still walked to the entrance of the TV room to greet them out of politeness. Then I quietly had my dinner alone in the dining room. In my mind I really wanted to join them, but I just dared not. The TV room seemed like a private area for them. I didn't want to invade their personal territory because I knew Americans valued privacy a lot.

The following days and weeks they had dinner in the TV room, and I felt like I was an outsider, not knowing how to fit myself into their life. I tried to talk with them, but somehow it seemed there was little in common between their lives and mine. Our conversations always revolved around nothing but their dog and cat. Especially my interaction with Mr. Harris really frustrated me. Very often, he would just mind his own business without saying anything even when I passed by. The way he acted made me feel as if I were invisible.

For the first month, as long as I stayed at the house, I felt very cautious. I dared not touch anything outside my room. If I had to use something, such as pot or pan, I would try my best to clean it. I also dared not make any sound even in my own room. Since the house was in the residential area, it was extremely silent, especially at night. I had my TV caption on all the time. I told my friends not to call me after 11:00.

Everyday routines at the house became grueling. I knew their schedule very well. Both Mr. and Mrs. Harris worked from 8 AM to 5 PM on weekdays, but they had a short lunch break at home to let the dog out in the backyard. My entire schedule changed to follow theirs. After they left for work, I forced myself to get up despite I wasn't an early bird. I would cook, do my laundry, and do other chores. Before they came back for lunch, I went to the university. After my classes finished, it was around 3:30. I would rush back to the house to make use of the remaining time to cook and eat. When they returned home, I would run to my room as quickly as I could, pretending that I was studying too hard to socialize with them, and then stay at my room all night. Sometimes, if I didn't have my supper before they came back, I would rather suffer from hunger at my room than go down to get a bite because I had to pass by the TV room on the way to the kitchen. I felt tired of this hide-and-seek game, but I didn't know how to change.

Then, one evening I got home late and went to my room without eating. I was very hungry and tired. I sat on my bed in despair when suddenly I started to cry. "This isn't like I expected," I said sadly to myself. "How can my life be like this? No friendly smiles. No long interesting conversations. No meals together."

At that moment I realized I had to change the way I interacted with them. I tried to create more opportunities to hang out with them. Instead of always locking myself at my room, I let my door open so that I could chat with them if they passed by. On weekend, I cooked Chinese food for them. When Mrs. Harris was doing housework, I offered her help. Little by little, we were getting more and more familiar.

Then one day Mr. and Mrs. Harris invited me to walk the dog in a near woods. That was the first time I was invited to join them. I was so excited! When hiking in the woods, they discussed about the plants and flowers along the trails. Although the terminologies were all Greek to me, I still tried to join their conversation once in a while by saying something simple like, "These flowers are beautiful."

A few days later, after helping Mrs. Harris with housework, she invited me to dinner with her and her husband in the TV room, which I had always hoped for! We had our dinner and watched a thriller together. When I couldn't understand, I just followed their facial expressions. They frowned, I frowned. They screamed. I screamed. After the movie, I sort of felt like I was an insider, and I found out Mr. Harris actually was very humorous sometimes.

We had many meals in the TV room, walks in the woods, and even long chats in the kitchen. My dream had come true to interact with locals in an American town. I will keep this special experience in my heart forever. But, the path to fulfilling that dream was not easy. I had to understand and face myself and my false impression about how local Americans interact, as well as challenge myself to open up my heart and adjust my own way of interacting with them. ∎

A Polite Confrontation—
A Student from Colombia
Confronts Her American Roommate

The next narrative shows how an exchange student from Colombia confronted her American roommate. Her roommate made noise late at night, and she had "romantic situations" in the room with her boyfriend. Such behavior greatly annoyed this international student. So she thought about her roommate's behavior, her own values in relation to this behavior (especially the boyfriend spending the night), as well as how she should confront her roommate. Her thoughtful approach to solving the problem worked.

I moved into Fischer Hall about two months ago, and I still miss things in my home. To have my own bathroom, my own space, to have in a certain way that peace I cannot feel these days. But, is better now after I talked with my roommate. I even like her now.

For the first month it was hard to get along with my roommate. She is very active and stays up late at night. I like to go to bed early. She constantly woke me. One day I went to bed very early because I felt very tired. I was sleeping very pleasant when I felt her knocking on the door. I woke up with a big effort and opened the door. She said she had left the keys inside, but she did not apologize because of the interruption. She opened the refrigerator and made noise for about five minutes and then went out of the room again. That made me feel bad but I did not have time to say anything.

I went back to sleep after some effort, but woke up again when she came into the room. This time she was giggling and talking with her boyfriend. I pretended to sleep, but I heard them talking. Then, he left, and I could sleep. But, the next morning I felt very tired.

A few days later I entered the room, and she was with her boyfriend in a very "romantic" situation. I put on my backpack in my bed and went out again doing like if I had not noticed anything.

I decided to talk with her that same day, but first I thought about the problem. For American girls like her, it is alright to sleep with their boyfriends in the dorm room. But, for me is strange. Even though it is strange for me,

I know this is not my country. So, I did not want to insult her or make her feel bad. So, I knew I had to be careful the way I talk to her but I also had to let her know how I feel.

Later that day I saw her, and I explained to her that my culture was not so open minded, and that for me, was not easy to accept she could have sex in the same place I was living. I tried to be the most direct I could be, but indeed I was very afraid of her reaction.

She understood what I was asking—privacy. Since that time, she did not bring her boyfriend to the room anymore. I think it was the best decision for her and for me. She uses the room to study and watch TV, but she leaves when I want to sleep. And, we talk sometimes. She is very nice to me, and we can talk in a friendly roommate way.

There are so many things that an exchange student has to adapt to if she wants to succeed in this experience. But, this does not mean that she has to accept also the things that does not like. The roommates of foreign students are very important support for the people that are in new environment. We need their understanding with this new situation to be comfortable here. ■

"Give Me Five, Bro!"— A Student from South Korea Becomes Aware of His Prejudices and Makes New Friends

The next narrative illustrates how a student gains awareness of his prejudices through a misperceived frightening encounter with an African American in an elevator at a department store. The young student was able to successfully reflect on this experience and to change his perceptions.

I am going to tell you about an experience I had while adjusting to life in the United States. This incident, I believe, was caused by cultural misunderstanding. The incident happened approximately two years ago after I first came to United States from Korea. One day I went to a department store in a shopping mall. I had to go up to the fourth floor to buy something there. When I got into the elevator, there were only an African-American man and me. He was standing in front of the floor numbers, so I asked him, "Could you press number four for me?"

The African-American guy surprised me with his reply! He held out his hand and said, "Give me five, bro!"

I suddenly became afraid, and when the elevator stopped on the fourth floor, I reached into my wallet, my hand shaking, and gave the man five dollars. As soon as the elevator's door opened, I ran out quickly to the men's restroom. The African-American guy followed me even to the men's room. I thought he wanted more money, so I gave him five more dollars.

The guy stood with his mouth wide open and my money in his hand. He then looked at me with wide eyes, frowned, gave the money back to me, and said, "No sweat, bro." He walked out.

I was so surprised by this incident I stayed in the men's room looking at myself in the mirror. "What just happened?"

When I got back to my apartment, I used Google to look up "Give me five, bro." I learned that it means "high-five," a gesture to greet another person. It means "good fellowship or triumph."

The high-five greeting is not a common thing you can see in Korea, and evidently at that time I did not know what the high-five was. And, the incident really made me think! I remembered the encounter with the African-American many times in the next few days. I also talked about the experience with other Korean students. It became obvious to me that I had a prejudice against African-American men at that time. Why did I think the guy wanted money from me? It was prejudice. I thought he wanted to rob me!

I felt very bad. But, I now understand that, first of all, it is very unusual for Koreans to talk to a stranger in public place. I now know it is quite common in America for people to say "Hi" or "Good morning" to anybody they encounter during their morning walk, or to strike up a conversation with another person waiting in line. If you said "Hello" or "Good morning" to a stranger in Korea, you would be looked upon as a rather odd person.

I also realize now that I never had a chance to talk to African-American people before. So, I did not know how to interact with them. I also think I saw too many old Hollywood action movies back in Korea before I came to the United States. In old Hollywood action movies the African-American guys often belong to the bad party. I think this is changing now, though. There are now many African Americans who are the good guys. I am happy about that. Maybe other Koreans won't have such a negative impression of African Americans.

I have adjusted now, and I have some African-American friends. When I tell them this story, they think it is very funny. But, they also agree with me that to understand people from other cultures, we need to appreciate their diversity and keep an open mind. ■

The Special Gift— A Student from China Learns about Gift Wrapping and When to Open Presents

The next narrative not only demonstrates reflection and action on the part of a student from China, but also highlights another point: Some things that seem insignificant to a person from one culture, can hold great importance to someone from another culture.

B efore I came to the States, I was advised to take some typical Chinese gifts, such as handkerchiefs, paper fans, and paper cuts. I was told that Western people give presents to each other during Christmas and birthdays and at other times.

In China people also like to give gifts to each other, especially to celebrate Chinese New Year. People often visit each other carrying cakes or apples or other fruits packed in shops. As far as I know, in the past no one took pains to wrap the gifts, but more recently some shops and department stores wrap fruits in cellophane and beautiful bows. Where I grew up, family and friends didn't expect gifts to be wrapped so beautifully, and so when I was invited to an American home for Christmas, I didn't think very much about how I would wrap my present. I simply put the paper fans and paper cuts in crisp new bags. But, I soon discovered that in other cultures how the present is wrapped is as important as the gift itself! I also discovered a different way to give and receive presents.

My good friend Sachiko, from Japan, has a host family, and they invited her, me, and another Japanese friend, Yuki, to eat Christmas dinner and enjoy the holiday with them. Soon after we arrived, we sat in the living room, admiring the big beautiful Christmas tree. Then, Sachiko's Uncle Frank's daughter presented each of us with Christmas gifts in beautiful wrapping paper. Sachiko, in front of all the people, took off the wrapping paper and opened the gift and said how nice a gift it was and thanked them, and I followed her example as I had no experience opening presents in front of everyone.

Then, it was our turn to give gifts, and Sachiko and Yuki took beautifully wrapped presents out of the big colorful bags they were carrying and gave them to the host family. I hesitated, feeling shy and embarrassed to present my gifts as they were not wrapped. Suddenly all my gifts became embarrassing, as if a little girl was presented to guests without a dress on.

But, everyone could see I was embarrassed, and they were so nice to me. They praised the presents with cheerful voices: "Oh! What beautiful intricate paper cuttings! How do they make these? How interesting!"

We had a wonderful Christmas evening. We ate an American Christmas dinner, ate lots of Christmas cookies, sang Christmas songs, and talked about our countries and families. We all felt very relaxed and thankful for a wonderful time.

Later that night, in my apartment, I laid on my bed thinking about the evening. I learned many things, including lots of new words, like *Christmas tree ornaments*, *sand tarts* [cookies], and *holly*. I also learned how to open a gift in an American way in front of everyone. I also learned a valuable lesson about the importance of wrapping gifts. To be frank with you, in China I was told that Americans wrap gifts, but I didn't take it seriously. From now on, I will definitely wrap my gifts to Americans and to Japanese friends!

But, the most important thing I learned was that the Americans I met that night were very nice to me when

I was embarrassed. When I felt very uncomfortable as I took my unwrapped presents out from my bag, everyone made me feel less and less awkward, even happy, because they loved the gifts. I now know that although the wrapping paper is an important part of the ceremony of giving a Christmas present, the wrapping paper itself is not as important as the person presenting the present. And, this lesson is the most special gift of all. ■

Being Heard—A Hesitant Student from Japan Devises Ways to Join in Class Discussions

The final narrative shows a reflective student who creates personal goals and develops strategies to ask the professor questions and to participate in small group discussions.

When I attended classes as an exchange student, I was confused. I did not understand how I should behave there. I suffered from not only having to understand the content of the books, but also how to behave, learn, and join in the class. I encountered various aspects that are totally different from Japanese classes. I had a hard time, and I realized I had to learn how to adjust to this American classroom life.

I had predictions of American classrooms. I thought students would be noisier than Japanese students. A professor could be more friendly compared to Japanese professors. Even though I would encounter small differences, at least, I thought I would be fine because I prepared well for class.

But, during the first few weeks, I knew there was something wrong with my expectations. I was surprised when one of my classmates was late to class and walked in front of the teacher and sat down without an excuse. It was also hard for me to believe that the students chewed gum and drank pop during the class. Surprisingly, the professor did not seem to care. She just kept talking. I was amazed that the students stopped her lecture whenever they had questions and their own opinions to share. The professor was glad to answer their questions, it seemed, and to respond and discuss their opinions. Even she encouraged the students to do this, I felt. All I could do is sit in silence, listening and watching. Even thinking about asking a question made me nervous.

In one of my smaller seminar courses, the professor had us talk in small groups. She did this in every class, and I had a big problem. To begin, I could not process the questions that the professor gave to us to answer in our groups as fast as the American students. By the time I understood the question, the students were well into the discussion. The only thing I could do was nod. I was depressed because I wanted to join in, but I could not. I was irritated at my language disability.

These surprises made me think. I thought that if I behaved like a good Japanese student, I would not have any trouble. Like in Japan, I expected to keep quiet in class except to answer the teacher's questions, if he asked questions. I also expected, like in Japan, to seldom give my own opinion. Like in Japan, I didn't expect to ask the teacher questions in class. If students have questions, they are likely to ask them after class because they don't want to disturb the teacher. I knew I had to overcome my limitations. I realized my abilities in English were not equal to the American students. I had to take action.

I decided first to solve my problem with my fear of talking in class. I pushed myself to raise my hand. This was very very hard for me to do. When I did raise my hand the first time, I was so nervous that I don't even know what I said! The professor pointed at me, and I started to talk. I was extremely tired even though I took less than 10 seconds. My feelings were mixed. I felt nervousness, embarrassment, shyness, and anxiety. I also felt good because I did it. Then, after talking in class several times, I realized that the more I spoke, the more confidence I would gain.

I also planned to talk during small group activities. Here is one of the ways I used. Sometimes the professor gave a list of questions for us to answer in our groups. I knew that I could not understand the questions as fast as the Americans. I also knew that the students would read all the questions before they began to discuss the answer to the first one. So, I read the first question, and then I thought about what I was going to say to my classmates. I didn't worry about the rest of the questions. Then, when we started to talk about the first question, I made sure to jump in right away and to be the first person to talk. After I explained my opinion, other students asked me to say more, and they gave their opinion. Then, when they started discussing the second question, I read the third question and gave my opinion right away.

At the end of the semester, I was still embarrassed and irritated because sometimes my speech did not have any conclusion or what I said did not make sense. Although I knew that I could not be the same as American student, I could say my own opinion and behave like American student sometimes, and I was happy about this. ■

CHAPTER 14

Finding Support

In addition to using humor and optimism, observing and matching behavior, and doing and reflecting as strategies for successful adjustment, international students seek support with the university and community as a way to adapt. Students often seek out a support network from international student organizations on campus, writing and learning centers, professors, foreign student advisors, academic advisors, new friends and classmates (foreign and American), host family members, church groups, and neighbors.

It is outside the scope of this chapter to address all the ways that international students make use of the university and local communities to develop a support network and help them to adjust to a new social and academic setting. As a result, the two narratives in this chapter only look at two ways students find support—through study groups and professors.

 ## The Power of a Study Group — A Student from Taiwan Gains Confidence in Writing and Speaking English

The first narrative shows how a stressed student finds the support she needs through a study group.

have been here for over two years. I will graduate with MBA in two weeks. It is so strange, in some ways, though. It seems like only yesterday I came here. I can remember it so clearly.

As soon as I arrive, everything was so different from my expectations! The most difficult part for me happened in the classroom. I thought I might have problems with speaking, but I did not think have so many problems with reading and writing. But, this was not the case! I had lot of problems with everything!

The classes were small with about 15 students in each class. As I was studying in international MBA program, there were mixture of American and international students in each class. The first day in class every teacher wanted us to introduce ourselves. Everyone introduce themselves in confident way, including other international students. But, I was so nervous. My voice so soft the professor told me, "Speak louder." This only made me more nervous. I was very surprised I was so nervous to introduce myself in public. In Taiwan, never nervous about speaking up in class.

During first few weeks I could hardly speak at all. The professors had whole-class discussions, and sometimes they put us in small groups. Most students spoke a lot. But, I just sat looking down at my notebook. Before each class began, I told myself, "Just say something; it's not difficult. You just need to speak something." But, it didn't work well. I couldn't speak, even though I really wanted to. I felt so upset.

I also had big problem with reading and writing, which surprised me, like I said before. To be honest it was first time in my life to have more than one textbook in class. Each professor assigned several chapters from several different books for us to read before each class.

"No way," I shouted to myself. "It is impossible to finish reading so much in such short time!" But, I struggled to complete all reading before each class.

We had to write bi-weekly papers in my basic introduction to business course. I spent many hours writing the first paper. I even went to university writing center to consult with a writing tutor. But, I got my paper back from the professor with a low grade and a note to go to writing center for help. "I can't believe it! I already went there!" It made me very upset. I even cried on my way to my apartment.

I didn't know how I can deal with my problems and assignments. I felt angry one minute, sad few minutes later, and sleepy few minutes later! I couldn't sleep, and I start to criticize everything and everyone, especially professors.

I was feeling very bad, but one night, I felt calm. I knew I had to be strong and try my best. After all, I came here to learn and improve my ability. I decided to find help. I was sort of friendly with one American girl in two of my courses, and I asked her if I can study with her sometime. She told me she has a study group with two other American students. She invited me and another international student in MBA program to join them.

At the beginning the five of us met on Sunday, but soon we met three times a week. We read in silence, and we talked about what we read. As we talked, I realized that American students don't always understand the reading, and I was partly shocked and partly happy when I can explain meaning of complex reading to American student. I also learned that I need to read differently. I stopped trying to understand every word. Instead, I paid attention to main idea in the reading and how the author support or defended these ideas. I soon discovered I can read faster and understand more this way.

In one class, students had to do research and give oral presentation on what we learned. My friends in our study group were really helpful in this respect. We would practice our presentation, give feedback and suggestions, and offer encouragement. I am sure this made a big difference in the quality of our classroom presentations.

As for my writing, I still struggled. But, I went to the writing center several times as I wrote my papers. Then, after I had wrote many drafts, I gave my paper to two members of the study group. The American helped a lot to fix my poor grammar, and this helped me a lot. But, the most surprising thing for me was I got some very useful suggestions from the international student, and I learned I can give thoughtful suggestions, too.

Although I only got a B on second paper in the Introduction class, I got A+ on my third paper with wonderful comments from professor. I also earned high evaluation on my classroom presentations.

I ended my first semester with a B and three A's. I also made good friends. But, as important I think, I gained confidence in myself, and I discovered when I need to be strong, I can be strong. I also learned that study group can be valuable, especially when members are cooperative and understanding. ■

A Talk with My Professor— A Student from Kenya Explains How His Essay Reflects His Cultural Values

The next narrative illustrates how a young student was able to win the trust and interest of an open-minded professor.

During my freshman year, I took a course called College Writing, and we were asked to analyze a movie that we watched. I thought it was a film about some guy trying to get some girl to do sexual things with him, and there were some provocative passionate scenes with partial nudity, some of them in public places. I wrote my paper, and I explained that I didn't like the film because it was too explicit. I mean there are some things you do in public. There are some things you don't do in public. I wrote my paper from a Kenyan view. But, I think many Americans are used to seeing a lot of public display of sexual things, so that was okay for them. They could see romance, and students who wrote about romance got a high grade. But, I didn't see a romantic movie. I saw a lot of public display of sex. So, I got a low letter grade for that paper.

I think the teacher didn't know my Kenyan background. She didn't know where I was coming from. So I went to see her about the grade, and after I explained it to her, she was like, "Oh! That makes sense." She listened to me when I explained to her my background and why I thought the movie was not romantic, but simply a lot of sexual display.

We talked about the paper and how I can explain my point of view more clearly by adding more about my Kenyan background. Then, she let me rewrite the paper. She changed my grade to an A. I really like that teacher. I respect her because she cares about students and who we are, and wants us to learn. ∎

PART 5
REFLECTIVE QUESTIONS

1. Which adaptation strategies do you find the most interesting? Why?

2. One of the narratives in Chapter 11 illustrates how a Syrian couple used humor to teach a little boy about their culture. Another narrative in Chapter 11 shows how a Saudi Arabian student used an optimistic attitude during his stay in the United States. What do you think of these narratives? How did humor and goodwill act as strategies that led to harmonious communication?

3. One problem facing international students is that observation across cultures is immensely difficult. Storti (2001) explains: "The trouble is that you will not be able to see anything that does not constitute *meaningful behavior* in your own culture" (p. 80). Is Storti correct? If Storti is correct, and it is enormously difficult to perceive behavior that is not a part of our experience, then how is it possible for students to adapt?

4. The narratives in Chapter 12 illustrate how some students used observation and matching behavior as a strategy to adapt to American culture. What other behavior can international students observe and possibly imitate? Include both verbal and nonverbal behavior.

5. Try these matching techniques. Then talk to someone who also has tried them. What did you learn from the experience? Consider how matching behavior can be used as a way for you to adapt to another culture.

   - Sit next to someone from another culture. Match this person's posture, gestures, facial expressions, and breathing.

   - Sit in the middle of a movie theater. Do whatever the audience does. Laugh when they laugh. Sigh when they sigh. Sit the way they sit.

- Find someone from a cultural background different from your own. Follow this person as he or she walks. Try to match pace, stride, way of moving through a crowd, and other aspects of walking.

- Watch people doing things, such as buying something at a store, getting a waiter's attention, eating an ice cream cone, counting on fingers, or eating soup. Try to match their way of doing things.

6. The narratives in Chapter 13 show that international students who try to reflect on and evaluate their experiences, as well as generate and try out alternative ways of interacting based on their reflections, will steadily adapt, and will eventually gain strong intercultural communication abilities in the new culture. How do the narratives in this chapter support this idea? What thoughts do you have about the importance of doing, reflecting, and changing behavior as a way to adapt?

7. How did the study group provide support for the Taiwanese student (Chapter 14)? Have you ever been a part of a study group? How did it provide chances for you to advance your knowledge and abilities?

8. What are ways that a university community can support international students?

9. Weaver (2000b) provides several ways to reduce the strong feelings associated with culture shock. These strategies include "transferring potent reminders from one's home culture," such as photographs and favorite CDs (p. 85). Other strategies are to share feelings with others who have experienced cultural adaptation and to use relaxing techniques (meditation, exercise). What other strategies can you think of?

PART 6

Home Again—Readapting and Reflections on Living Abroad

Part 6 focuses on issues related to readjusting to the home culture and on reflections international students have about their lives after they complete their stay in the United States. Chapter 15 addresses the problems that some students from Russia, Korea, Indonesia, and Thailand have had soon after returning home. Chapter 16 focuses on the kind of self-awareness that some returning students from Russia and Kazakhstan say they gained about themselves and their cultures after adapting to life in the United States.

CHAPTER 15

Problems Readjusting to the Home Culture

When students return to their home countries after studying abroad, it is not uncommon for them to experience difficulties in readjusting because of changes they have made in their values, attitudes, and behavior, as the narratives in this chapter illustrate.

Have I Become an Outsider? — A Russian Returnee Questions Her Identity in Her Native Country

The first narrative illustrates the kinds of problems some students have when they return to their home countries after being away for years. The Russian returnee, who had at least partially taken on an American identity, questions whether she had become an outsider in her native country and explains that she did not appreciate the serious and remote Russian style of interaction.

> I am now married to an American and live here in the United States, and I am well adjusted to American life. I am very happy. Thinking about it, I have always been happy here, even when I was a high school student (at

a private school) and undergraduate in America. I don't remember ever having any culture shock at all. I was actually happy all the time.

However, I did have culture shock when I went back to Russia after living for ten years here. One of the problems in Russia I had was I think in English. I rarely used Russian here in the States. All my friends were and still are Americans. So, I'd say for instance, my written English is much better than my written Russian. Then there were other things, like, when I spoke Russian in Russia, it was kind of funny. I spoke Russian with an American accent, so people didn't understand what I said. For instance, I was in Moscow, and I wanted to buy a computer, a laptop. So I went to different places that sell computers, and the moment I started talking, people would immediately switch to English. They automatically thought that I was an American. When I spoke Russian, people didn't recognize it as Russian! It was so cool.

But, soon I started to experience shock, mostly because of the way people speak, the way people do things in Russia. Russians are not really friendly, generally speaking; people rarely smile. They are quite serious. It's kind of hard to explain. So, I didn't enjoy talking with Russians, even when they got beyond my American accent. I missed all the friendly smiles and chats in America.

And also, immediately after they heard the American accent, for instance, I think they labeled me as an outsider. And what is sort of interesting is that my parents planned that for me initially by sending me to school in America. I don't feel sad about that; it is wonderful.

I live in America now, but I still consider myself a native Russian. I mean English is one of the languages that I speak, but I do not think the status of Americans is higher. Now, whenever I visit Russia, I do not feel sad about Russians thinking I am an outsider because I like to piss them off [laugh]. ■

Why Are You Still Single?—After 10 Years of Living Abroad, a Korean Returnee Is Faced with Endless Personal Questions

The next narrative shows a different kind of readjustment problem. This female student spent ten years living and studying in the United States. When she returned after completing her doctoral degree, she faced many different problems that led to reentry shock, and she associates many of these problems with being a woman and unmarried. Her narrative provides a partial view into her reentry problems and process.

I was so shocked and mortified when a young lady asked, "Why are you still single?" during the first week after I returned to my country from the States. Although I knew that many women who are still single in their late 30s or older would face this question as a greeting in my country, still I was shocked. I was not ready to receive this kind of greeting. I wanted to reply, "That's none of your business!" However, over and over again, I am and will be greeted with that question as soon as anybody finds out my age.

I knew I would not like much about living back in my country in that I would be hearing this kind of greeting from everyone, even from my close family members. Probably, my family and relatives would be the most critical about my not yet marrying. In my country, if you are over 30 and single, then you give shame to your family, especially your parents. Here, when a woman is over 30, she is considered over the hill for marriage. The single woman becomes a big worry or burden to her family.

As soon as I landed in my country, I began to hear from so many people, almost everyone around me: "Why aren't you married?" "Do you have a boyfriend?" "Why don't you have someone to marry?" "When are you getting married?" "Don't you want to get married?"

On top of these uncomfortable greetings, people added another comment saying that since I received a degree in the States, I couldn't find a man. They said that because I was educated, I was never going to find any man who has a same degree as I do at my age. Although everyone laughed, all greetings to me seemed to be negative greetings. I understood that there are still humorously negative feelings in Korea in terms of women getting a higher education. However, at the moment when everyone was humorously asking me such personal questions, I didn't know whether I was laughing at their comments or laughing with them at me.

Since the airplane landed in my country, I have had countless experiences of being asked about my marital status. And it will not stop until I marry someone. I am very uncomfortable with such questions after being away from my country almost ten years. Tomorrow morning, I will go to see a doctor; definitely I will be asked about my marriage status by either a doctor or one of the nurses and then surely the follow-up questions: "Why aren't you married?" "Why are you still single?" ■

Things Are Different—An English Teacher from Indonesia Changes His Teaching Expectations after He Returns Home

The next narrative shows the kind of adaptation problems that students have with applying what they have learned in their university programs when they return to their countries. This student from Indonesia wants to create change in his community based on what he learned through his personal and academic experiences in the United States. But he soon realizes that the expectations and dreams he had in the U.S. about what his professional life would be after returning to Indonesia do not fit the realities he is facing at home.

Soon after I finished my academic TESOL program in the U.S., I was eager to prepare everything to go back to my home country, Indonesia. It seemed that I longed to see everyone after I had been away for about two years. I had attained my academic and personal dreams; completing a degree in the U.S. and bringing my academic success home, I was also expecting to share my knowledge, experiences, and viewpoints with everybody upon my return. In this sense, I believe that my experiences learning and living in the U.S. have changed my viewpoints, and so I expected that I will be able to contribute my knowledge, though to a small extent, to the development of my very own community in my home country.

Upon my arrival, however, I realized that things were not as easy as I thought they would be. I started to feel "shocked" when I looked around soon after I went out of my country's biggest airport. Although I used to be familiar with the surroundings before I went to the U.S., I could now see these surroundings with new eyes. For a quick example, I was very sorry to see many people smoked in public places (and ever worse, in air-conditioned rooms) and they did not seem to care about others around them. I, however, think that much of this action was due to people's ignorance. Raising people's awareness and stricter law enforcement will be helpful in helping reduce this problem.

Another kind of problem I experienced was when trying to explain to someone in my family to do or not to do something. I felt there were some kinds of conflicts in my head. For instance, I wanted to explain to Mother that we needed to manage our household wastes more wisely, but I felt that I might offend her by my somehow "Americanized" views (though that's not necessarily true). Within such culture that respects older people, it is advisable that younger ones respect and obey older people. It might be difficult to talk to older people and tell them things they might not like or do not agree with. So, I need to find the right moments or more judicious ways to let my older family members know about something.

I also find it difficult choosing what to do for a living upon my arrival. I was trained in the U.S. to be an English language teacher educator, and I expected to come back to Indonesia to educate pre-service or in-service teachers of English at one of our education and teacher training colleges in my hometown. In this regard, I was positively optimistic about getting a teacher education position. But, I was confronted by the fact that a teaching job would not be financially superior to other kinds of jobs. I was faced with a sort of dilemma where I have to choose between dedicating myself to teaching or working outside the education field.

I have decided to work as a teacher educator, but I will have to also work outside the university campus to earn extra money because a teaching job (almost anywhere in Indonesia) does not offer good money. On the basis of this, a lot of people decide to have multiple jobs in order to solve their financial problems. I am aware of this situation, a situation that requires me to step back and reflect on every decision I am going to make. It is one of my dreams to be able to contribute my knowledge to the development of English language teaching in my country, but I also have to think about maintaining and meeting my financial needs.

Regarding this particular dilemma, I think I have to manage my time more wisely so that I can both teach on campus and do some part-time job outside campus. I realize that working extra hours can riskily decrease my concentration in teaching but this is a kind of problem that I really have to pay attention and solve wisely.

Overall, my experiences readjusting into my own culture have brought about some frustration and disappointment because I cannot meet and get what I have expected ever since I left the United States. I know that I have some different viewpoints and want to make some changes, but I also have to be aware that changes will not come easily; more importantly, the changes that I wanted to see while studying in America are not necessarily the best answer to the problems I have been seeing after my arrival. I have to reconsider my approach and viewpoints so that I may appropriate them to the local contexts and deliver my messages more judiciously. When I am able to do this, people will likely listen to my messages. Hopefully! ■

Lost Love—A Student from Thailand Returns Home Early to Discover He Lost His True Love

The next narrative shows a different kind of problem, one that focuses on how others have changed at home while an international student has been in the United States and the effect this has had on the student after returning home. Here a student returned home after studying at a language institute in the United States for 18 months to discover that his girlfriend has changed and is no longer interested in continuing their relationship.

In Thailand I had a girl friend. We fell in love, and I wanted take care her. But, I had chance to go to United States to study English. It was not easy to go. My heart belonged to my girlfriend, but I also wanted to go America. You know what I mean?

In America I felt lucky—I learned a lot. I had friends, and I (learned) how to know Korea, Japan, Taiwan people. But, everyday I think about my girlfriend. I thought like this. I have very good chance to learn English in United States. Not everyone can study there. So, I want to study. But, I can't stop thinking about her.

So, I came back to take care of her. But, she changed, and she not want me anymore. This was big problem for me. My heart was weak. I had broken heart. My feeling was so so bad. Terrible. Very terrible. I could not do anything. I drank too much. No job. My mother, father worry too much. I wanted to be good son. But, I had broken heart. Broken heart.

Now, better life. I have good job and another girlfriend. My father and mother, happy. Life is good again. ■

CHAPTER 16

Awareness

Returning home is not simply and only about reentry challenges; for many international students it is also about fulfillment of goals and a new awareness about themselves, their individual cultural identities, and the world around them. Many international students return home feeling enriched from having learned to interact with Americans. They have added a new dimension to their identity, one that is uniquely American, and most are very much aware of the changes within them. Further, many international students have gained a considerable awareness about their own native cultures as a result of having lived in the United States.

The Right Decision—A Student from Russia Reflects on the Decisions She Made While Studying in the United States

The first narrative shows an exchange student's reflections about her stay in the United States after returning to her home country—what she learned about the process of cultural adaptation and what she discovered about herself.

At the beginning, I was full of fear. I don't know—it was a fear of making a mistake and being misunderstood. It was especially acute when I faced a native speaker. It was one thing to talk with Russian classmates in English in Russia who are in the same boat, and it is entirely different to open your mouth in front of a real English-speaking person. At least, this is how I thought before I went to America.

I had studied English in Moscow, and as I grew in my fluency within the Russian classroom, I gained more and more confidence in my English abilities. So, when I went to the United States during my junior year as an exchange student to a Kentucky college, I thought I was ready. However, upon arriving to America, I found myself in a vacuum. I could not understand students talking with one another—they talked too fast and used words I didn't know. I could not understand people in stores or at the post office—they spoke with a heavy accent; I even doubted sometimes whether or not it was English. I felt like a first-grader again! It took me some time to get tuned into the way people spoke, to learn the words they used, to change my own articulation. I cannot even start to tell you how many tears I shed in the process!

I had an American roommate, but we could not click for a long time. I did not feel very welcomed—we just had short and polite two- or three-line conversations about nothing. I expected her to reach out for me since I was a guest in her country, but she didn't. (Later she told me she was expecting me to make the first step, since it was I who had come to her country.) I felt alone even when I talked with the American girls in the dorm.

The strange thing is, when I first went to America everything seemed familiar to me: people looked the same, food looked the same, architecture was different, but it was not at all dramatic. But, the closer I looked, the more different things seemed. I tried some food I thought would taste sweet and it turns out salty. It was difficult to leave campus because I didn't have a car and there were no buses in the area, so I felt stuck. I discovered that people act in strange unpredicted ways. I think because things seemed the same as in Russia at first glance, but turned out to be so different, I felt very severe culture shock.

My immediate reaction was to find somebody in a similar situation, my fellow countrymen or other foreign students and stick together keeping defense against the alien world around us. We spent all our free time together, and it was actually fun for a while. We complained about Americans and things American, and we laughed at our bad jokes about Americans. But, I knew that this was wrong in a way and not why I came to America. Having gone through this isolated way of life, I can tell you it is not the most constructive way to survive. It helps at the initial stages, gives you strength not to go crazy, but then it starts to hold you back.

The hardest part for me was to make the decision to leave the security of the Russian community where I felt welcomed and to try to become more engaged in the American community. For strength I used the deep provoking feeling that I would regret it if I did not at least try to acclimate myself to America and make friends. I forced myself to socialize more with my roommate and her friends, and eventually we became good friends. We went to movies, restaurants, ice skating, and I even joined them on a trip to Florida for the spring break.

I returned home and finished my degree in Russia, and as I reflect on my experience in Kentucky, I can fully understand that I made the right decision. I have no regrets, and having crossed cultures, I have learned much about life itself.

To begin, if something is not the way it is in your own country, it is not automatically bad. As soon as you gain this awareness, you feel much more relieved. I have also realized it often takes a conscious effort to turn your mind the other way around, but if you manage to do this, you can learn to appreciate another culture, you learn its ways. You may still be trapped in the middle of nowhere, but now you know the difference between where you came from and the place you are. If you stay open to new experiences, you can enrich your knowledge of the world, as well as learn about yourself.

I especially learned that by accusing people in another culture of being ethnocentric, I ended up behaving in exactly the same way. When I made the decision to get to know Americans, rather than simply complaining that they think they are better than Russians, I was able to see that our cultures are simply different and people within America are also different. I know I made the right decision, one that opened my mind to understand and appreciate people in different cultures. ■

New Awareness—A Student from Kazakhstan Compares American Culture with Her Native Culture

The next narrative is from an interview with a graduate from a mid-sized state university. She talks about the awareness she gained about her own culture and identity. Her narrative is consistent with the thoughts of Weaver (2000a), who points out that "sojourners become more aware of what makes them different when they consciously examine culturally embedded values, beliefs, and thought patterns. They gain both greater awareness of their home culture and greater awareness of the individual 'self' and of what is important to them" (p. 200).

My first new awareness was actually during my first week here. I felt homesick. I missed my family and friends. I just wanted to pack my things and go back home. I even started to pack, and I called an agency to reserve an airline ticket home. Then, suddenly it struck me that in my culture if I go back home, people will say, "Oh, she couldn't study. That's why she came back. She already failed." You know, I became more aware at that moment that in my country we are society dependent and more family oriented. We take into account society's opinion. In Kazakhstan we should think about our family, people, neighbors, colleagues, everybody's opinions. We are not so individualistic like people in America.

You know, before I came to America, I always hated this—collectivism (as I have learned to call it while studying in America), about thinking about other people's opinion. But, in my situation it helped me because otherwise I would have gone home. Thinking about what other people would say, what my family would say, what my friends would say, it helped me. And, now I like this— my culture. It is part of who I am.

I started appreciating some cultural things in Kazakhstan. For example, I now appreciate the way children take care of their parents when they get old. Once I volunteered to talk with the elderly at a nursing home in the U.S., and I felt sorry for the elderly people. I can understand that the United States is a big country, and some children do take care of their parents when they are old. I also understand that children move away from their parents to work, and even if the children want to take care of their parents, some parents may not want to live with them. So their values are like this. I can understand this. I can also understand that in my culture it will be a disgrace for the family if we send our parents to some place like a nursing home. One of the children will take care of the parents when they get old. I think it is very good. But, before I lived in America and visited the nursing home, I didn't appreciate this.

I also became more aware about teaching possibilities. I am a teacher and came to the United States to develop myself as a teacher, and one thing I like in the U.S. is the way teachers treat you. Students feel free in the class to ask questions and even argue with the professor. In my country what the teacher says is right. You cannot argue with the professor. Another thing I like is that the professors in my courses were very busy, but whenever I asked them for help, they never said no. In my country, though, there is a big gap between the teacher and the student. I think in my country professors are more serious, and students are reluctant to speak to professors. But, I want to change this in my teaching. I will start teaching again soon, and I will try to make my relationship with the students close. It might be a little strange for the students at first, but I will encourage them to ask me questions and to talk with me freely. ■

PART 6
REFLECTIVE QUESTIONS ⩗⩗

1. Have you ever returned home after studying or living abroad for some time? Or have you known someone who returned home? What kind of readjustment problems did you or he or she have?

2. What is the "right decision" that the Russian student made while studying in the United States? How difficult do you think it is to make such a decision?

3. What kind of new awareness did the student from Kazakhstan gain from her experience in the United States? What other kinds of awareness can be gained from living in another culture?

4. What does Weaver (2000a) mean when he says: "Most (international students) will actually experience more stress during reentry than during their entry into another culture. Those who adjusted best and were the most successful overseas usually experience the greatest amount of difficulty with reverse culture shock" (p. 221)?

Conclusion

The personal narratives throughout this book illustrate the challenges, difficulties, and successes experienced by international students studying at colleges and universities in the United States. Through the narratives, the international students explain—in their own words—their cultural adaptation experiences related to these challenges, problems, and accomplishments.

As the international students' stories illustrate, cultural adaptation can be understood as a series of phases, including preparing to leave the home country for the United States, initial experiences in the U.S., increasing interaction and challenges, culture shock, and adaptation. Each phase is often associated with characteristic feelings—such as excitement, curiosity, and optimism during the students' initial experiences, and anxiety, homesickness, boredom, helplessness, self-doubt, and depression during the culture shock phase.

However, although understanding cultural adaptation as a set of phases is heuristically useful, cultural adaptation is not a linear set of phases but rather a recursive process for some international students, as the narratives in the book show. Cultural adaptation is also a recursive process in part because some international students experience value conflicts and identity issues even after they have been in the United States for awhile. This book featured stories, for example, by international students who faced challenges related to race and discrimination, as well as conflicting values in the use of time and what it means to be overweight.

The narratives in this book have also illustrated that some behaviors can encumber successful adaptation. The behaviors highlighted in this book included stories about students who continuously complain, avoid interaction with Americans, withdraw into the expatriate community, and expect Americans to adapt to their native home-culture way of interacting (or, more strongly, use an ethnocentric impulse that others are like them, and continue to expect other people to behave as they do).

However, as the students' narratives also illustrate, the majority of the international students used strategies that helped them to successfully adapt to college life and culture. The strategies accentuated in this book included students' use of humor and optimism, observation and behavior matching, and doing and reflecting.

Finally, the narratives at the end of the book have illustrated that the process of cultural adaptation does not end when students return home. As their narratives exemplify, some students have problems readapting to their home culture after completing their education in the United States because they have changed in ways that their friends and colleagues cannot understand and because their expectations of what they want to accomplish with their U.S. education does not match the realities of their home culture. However, the narratives at the end this book also illustrate that going through the process of cultural adaptation affords students chances to grow, to understand themselves, and to be able to perceive their own lives and their home culture in a different way.

As I wrote at the start of this book, the goal has been to illuminate the lives of international students who are studying at U.S. colleges and universities, and through the voices of the students to construct awareness about what it means to adapt to another culture. As such, to end this book, I leave you with two questions: What new awareness do you have about what it means to be and international student? How can you use this awareness?

References

Adler, P. The transitional experience: An alternative view of culture shock. *Journal of Humanistic Psychology 15* (4), 13–23, 1975.

Adler, P.S. "Culture Shock and the Cross-Cultural Learning Experience." In *Toward Internationalism*, eds. L.F. Luce and E.C. Smith, 24–35. Cambridge, MA: Newbury House, 1987.

Agar, M. *The Professional Stranger*. New York: Academic Press, 1980.

Agar, M. *The Professional Stranger*, 2nd edition. New York: Academic Press, 1996.

Anderson, P.A. and H. Wang. "Unraveling Culture Cues: Dimensions of Nonverbal Communication across Cultures." In *Intercultural Communication*, eds. L. Samovar, R.E. Porter, and E.R. McDaniel, 250–265. Belmont, CA: Thomson Wadsworth, 2006.

Arnold, J. and H.D. Brown. "A map of the Terrain." In *Affect in Language Learning*, ed. J. Arnold, 1–27. New York: Cambridge University Press, 1999.

Baker, C. "Membership Categorization and Interview." In *Qualitative Theory, Method, and Practice*, ed. D. Silverman, 162–176. London: Sage, 2004.

Bandler, R. and J. Grinder. *Frogs into Princes*. Moab, Utah: Real People Press, 1979.

Begley, P.A. "Sojourner Adaptation." In *Intercultural Communication*, eds. L. Samovar, R.E. Porter, and E.R. McDaniel, 387–393. Belmont, CA: Thomson Wadsworth, 2006.

Bennett, J.M. "Transition Shock: Putting Culture Shock in Perspective." In *Basic Concepts of Intercultural Communication*, ed. M.J. Bennett, 215–223. Yarmouth, ME: Intercultural Press, 1998.

Bennett, M.J. "Intercultural Communication: A Current Perspective." In *Basic Concepts of Intercultural Communication*, ed. M.J. Bennett, 1–34. Yarmouth, ME: Intercultural Press, 1998.

Bogdan, R.C. and S.K. Biklen. *Qualitative Research for Education*, 5th edition. Boston: Allyn and Bacon, 2006.

Brown, H.D. *Principles of Language Learning and Teaching*, 4th edition. White Plains, NY: Addison Wesley Longman, 2000.

Chong, N. and F. Baez. *Latino Culture*. Yarmouth, ME: Intercultural Press, 2005.

DeCapua, A. and A.C. Wintergerst. *Crossing Cultures in the Language Classroom*. Ann Arbor: The University of Michigan Press, 2004.

Denzin, N.K. and Y.K. Lincoln. *Handbook of Qualitative Research*. Thousand Oaks, CA: Sage, 1994.

Denzin, N.K. and Y.K. Lincoln. *Handbook of Qualitative Research*, 3rd edition edition. Thousand Oaks, CA: Sage, 2005.

Emerson, R., R. Freitz, and L. Shaw. *Writing Ethnographic Field Notes*. Chicago: University of Chicago Press, 1995.

Fanselow, J.F. "'Let's See': Contrasting Conversations about Teaching." *TESOL Quarterly 22*(1): 113–130, 1988.

Fanselow, J.F. "Post Card Realities." In *On Becoming a Language Educator*, eds. C.P. Casanave and S.R. Schecter, 157–172. Mahwah, NJ: Lawrence Erlbaum, 1997.

Furnham, A. and S. Bochner. *Culture Shock: Psychological Reactions to Unfamiliar Environments*. New York: Methuen, 1986.

Gebhard, J.G. What does it mean to be a Thai student at an American university? *PASAA: A Journal of Language Teaching and Learning in Thailand 17*(2): 13–21, 1987.

Gebhard, J.G. *Teaching English as a Foreign or Second Language: A Self-Development and Methodology Guide*. Ann Arbor: The University of Michigan Press, 1996.

Gebhard, J.G. Narrative research on culture shock: Sojourners' voices. International TESOL Conference, St. Louis (Paper), 2001.

Gebhard, J.G. *Teaching English as a Foreign or Second Language: A Self-Development and Methodology Guide,* 2nd edition. Ann Arbor: The University of Michigan Press, 2006.

Gebhard, J.G. "Asian international students' cultural adaptation at U.S. universities: Challenges, behaviors, and strategies." *English Language Teaching 22* (2): 21–53, 2010.

Giles, L. *A Study of Cultural Adjustment Processes of Latino Students at a Mid-sized State University*. Ph.D. Dissertation, Indiana University of Pennsylvania, 1996.

Grinder, J. and R. Bandler. *The Structure of Magic II*. Palo Alto, CA: Science and Behavior Books, 1976.

Grinder, J., J. DeLozier, and R. Bandler. *Patterns of Hypnotic Techniques of Milton H. Erickson*. Portland, OR: Metamorphous Press, 1996.

Hall, E.T. *The Silent Language*. New York: Doubleday and Company, 1959.

Hall, E.T. "The Power of Hidden Differences." In *Basic Concepts of Intercultural Communication*, ed. M.J. Bennett, 53–67. Yarmouth, ME: Intercultural Press, 1998.

Heinze, R.I. *Tham khwan: How to contain the essence of life*. Kent Ridge: Singapore University Press, 1982.

Klausner, W.J. and K. Klausner. *Communication or Conflict?* Bangkok: The Bangkok Post, 1970.

Klausner, W.J. *Reflections on Thai culture*. Bangkok: The Siam Society, 1993.

Kohls, R. *Survival Kit for Overseas Living*, 3rd edition. Yarmouth, ME: Intercultural Press, 2001.

Lewis, T.J. and Jungman, R.E. *On Being Foreign: Culture Shock in Short Fiction*. Yarmouth, ME: Intercultural Press, 1986.

Lincoln, Y. "Emerging Criteria for Qualitative Research." *Qualitative Inquiry* 1(3): 275–289, 1995.

Lysgaard, S. "Adjustment in a foreign society: Norwegian Fulbright grantees visiting the United States." *International Social Science Bulletin* 7: 45–51, 1955.

Maxwell, J.A. *Qualitative Research Design: An Interactive Approach*. Thousand Oaks, CA: Sage, 2004.

Morain, G.G. "Kinesics and Cross-cultural Understanding." In *Culture Bound*, ed. J.M. Valdes, 64–76. New York: Cambridge University Press, 1986.

Oberg, K. "Culture Shock: Adjustment to New Cultural Environments," *Practical Anthropology* 7 (1960): 177–178.

Ohata, K. *Cultural as well as Personal Aspects of Language Learning Anxiety: A Case Study of Seven Japanese Individuals' Reflective Accounts of Language Learning Anxiety*. Ph.D. Dissertation, Indiana University of Pennsylvania, 2004.

Pagnucci, G. *Living the Narrative Life: Stories as a Tool for Meaning Making*. Portsmouth, NH: Heinemann Boynton/Cook, 2004.

Purnell, D. *Cultural and Language Adjustment Processes of Taiwanese Students at a Small, Mid-Western College*. Ph.D. Dissertation, Indiana University of Pennsylvania, 2000.

Richards, K. *Qualitative Inquiry in TESOL*. New York: Palgrave Macmillan, 2003.

Rosen, S.L. *My Voice Will Go with You: The Teaching Tales of Milton H. Erickson*. New York: W.W. Norton, 1982.

Ruben, B.D. "Guidelines for Cross-cultural Communication Effectiveness." In *Toward Internationalism*, eds. L.F. Luce and E.C. Smith, 36–46. New York: Newbury, 1987.

Rubin, H.J. and I.S. Rubin. *Qualitative Interviewing: The Art of Hearing Data*, 2nd edition. Thousand Oaks, CA: Sage, 2004.

Rule, R. and S. Wheeler. *True Stories: Guidelines for Writing about Your Life*. New Portsmouth, NH: Heinemann Boynton/Cook, 2000.

Scovel, T. The effect of affect on foreign language learning: A review of the anxiety research. *Language Learning 28*, 129–142, 1978.

Singer, M.R. "Culture: A Perceptual Approach." In *Basic Concepts of Intercultural Communication*, ed. M.J. Bennett, 97–110. Yarmouth, ME: Intercultural Press, 1998.

Spradely, J.P. *The Ethnographic Interview*. New York: Holt, Rinehart & Winston, 1979.

Storti, C. *The Art of Crossing Cultures*. Yarmouth, ME: Intercultural Press, 1989.

Storti, C. *The Art of Crossing Cultures*, 2nd edition. Yarmouth, ME: Intercultural Press, 2001.

Storti, C. *The Art of Coming Home*. Yarmouth, ME: Intercultural Press, 1996.

Tambiah, S. J. *Buddhism and the Spirit Cults of Northeast Thailand*. Cambridge: Cambridge University Press, 1970.

Wang, M.M., Brislin, R., Wang, W-Z, Williams, D., and Chao, J.H. 2000. *Turning Bricks into Jade: Critical Incidents for Mutual Understanding Among Chinese and Americans*. Yarmouth, ME: Intercultural Press, 2000.

Weaver, G. "The Process of Reentry." In *Culture, Communication and Conflict*, ed. G.R. Weaver, 220–228. New York: Pearson Publishing, 2000a.

Weaver, G. "Understanding and Coping with Cross-cultural Adjustment Stress." In *Culture, Communication and Conflict*, ed. G.R. Weaver, 177–193. New York: Pearson Publishing, 2000b.

Wolfson, N. Compliments in cross-cultural perspective. In *Culture Bound*, ed. J. M. Valdes, 112–122. New York: Cambridge University Press, 1986.

Young, D.J. "A Perspective On Foreign Language Learning: From Body to Mind to Emotions." In *Affect in Foreign Language and Second Language Learning: A Practical Guide to Creating a Low-Anxiety Classroom Atmosphere*, ed. D.J. Young, 13–23. New York: McGraw Hill, 1999.